EVEN HERE

Finding God in Emotional and Mental Suffering

Ben Willey

Common Life

For a corresponding sermon series that went along with the release of *Even Here* visit www.fellowshipsj.org.

Bible References are used from the English Standard Version and the New International Version.

THE HOLY BIBLE, English Standard Version. Wheaton, IL: Crossway. 2016 Edition. THE HOLY BIBLE, New International Version, NIV Copyright 1973, 1978, 1984, 2011 by Biblica Inc.

All stories with included names have been used with the permission and correct name of the individual that is portrayed. Some stories are used that do not have specific information to identify individuals involved.

 *Common Life* resources is a literature ministry of Fellowship Community Church in Mt. Laurel and Collingswood, NJ. Team members contributed to the title, cover design, editing and proofreading of *Even Here*. Lisa Meyers gave a significance investment of her time and talent in conversation, edits and design of the project.

REVIEWS

"What I found was not light but a companionship in the dark." As a fellow OCD-sufferer, these words leapt off the page and seized me by the shoulders. I've been there. I know this. Which makes me incredibly grateful for this book. Ben Willey writes with courageous honesty, a compelling compassion, and seasoned wisdom. This is no formulaic how-to manual for sufferers; it is far better. It is a tender and much-needed invitation to find Christ in the darkness of our suffering.

> - *Bob Stevenson, Lead Pastor at Aurora Bible Church and Gospel Coalition Author. Aurora, IL.*

Even Here: Finding God in Emotional and Mental Suffering by Ben Willey is a Biblical and historical exploration of the Christian experience of suffering. Through his own experiences, Ben shares his transformative journey as he's learned to lean into Jesus' care; it's a journey that will reorient your spirit and give a better definition to your suffering. Ben's wisdom provides comfort and reassurance, reminding us that in our darkest times, we are never forsaken by God or isolated in our struggles. This book is an invaluable companion for anyone seeking to find God's presence amid life's most challenging moments.

> - *Christ Katulka. Radio Host and Director of North American Ministries at Friends of Israel and Author of The Common Thread. Haddonfield, NJ.*

Ben writes from a place of deep understanding and personal experience of ongoing suffering. Through his own journey with darkness, God has met him time and again with compassion and tenderness, revealing powerful insights. These are not neat and tidy solutions wrapped up in a pretty bow. Rather, they are treasures discovered in the unending shadows of darkness, learned through struggle and despair.

This is a book for everyone: for those who battle with the weariness of chronic suffering, they will find a companion who truly understands, and comfort that they are not alone. For those who have friends or family members who face ongoing struggles, they will gain greater compassion and perspective as they journey alongside them.

Ben's writing is honest and vulnerable. He does not hold back from sharing difficult truths learned along the way, but does it with respect and humility. We need authors like Ben who are willing to tell it like it is, guiding us gently through places of discomfort, confusion, and avoidance.

> - *Lisa Skopil, Co-director of The Leadership Institute School of Spiritual Direction and Author at The Leadership Institute. Orange, CA.*

To speak from the depths of a soul experience is the richest of voices. Ben's voice is gold. Insights into the reality of life lived as God intends does not preclude pain, misfortune, and difficulty. We crave the light but it must include the dark. Ben knows because he's been there. "God's companionship in the dark is the primary treasure found in the dark." (from chapter One) Ben Willey understands abundant life lived with emotional and psychological darkness. Read this book if you want to learn how to carry your cross daily!

> - *Dr. Craig Babb, EdD. Founder and Director of Rhythm of Grace Ministries. Prairie Village, KS.*

Ben Willey has provided here a unique book for Christians who experience the struggle of Mental Illness and the shame that often comes with it. Personal, practical, and insightful while also being well-researched, Even Here is an accessible companion and guide to those experiencing emotional and mental suffering.

> - *Dr. Matthew Miller, PsyD. Clinical Director of Center for Christian Counseling and Relational Development.*

Marlton, NJ.

Ben Willey illuminates both what people understand about others and what they understand about themselves. Writing of this quality comes from a true commitment to listening, and from a perfect attunement to the human condition. He is a brilliant chronicler of the ambiguity and the delicacy of the human condition.

    - Joan Kings, Psychiatric Nurse Practitioner. Doylestown, PA.

Ben Willey has written more than a book, but also a traveling companion that come alongside of all who walk the weighty roads of mental, emotional and spiritual struggle. He writes from experience, as one who has traversed dark valleys and has encountered God's comforting presence in that place. This book will serve as an encouragement to many, reminding them that they are not alone— God hears them, sees them and is in the valley with them.

    - Dr. Eric Rivera, PhD. Associate Professor of Pastoral Theology at Trinity Evangelical Divinity School, Lead Pastor at The Brook (Chicago), Author of Unexpected Jesus. Chicago, IL.

I loved this book. I had to read it in small increments within the nooks and crannies of my full life. Every time I read a bit, I wanted to keep reading. I am excited to hear a pastor be so candid. Ben is both transparent and courageous in writing this book. I know his honest personal story, the examples of pilgrims who've gone before us, as well as the practical tools shared will greatly benefit anyone who reads it. I think this book is for you, the reader, as much as it is for those you love and serve. I am excited to share copies of it!

    - Joanne Sharp, Founder of Encouragher Ministries and Author of Seeking Rest. Medford, NJ.

Dedication

To Jesus and Adriana, the Author and
quill of my messy faith.
To Atticus of courage,
Solomon of peace,
Eden of flourishing and
Cielo of light -
In this world and in each of us there is
much fear and love.
Pursue love.

CONTENTS

x

Prayer of entrance:

I'm trying to be here. Yes, here.
Here, in this place of mental and emotional pain.
I'd rather meet you somewhere else. Anywhere else.
I don't want to be here with you because
it takes being here with myself, too.
I'd like to go somewhere less afraid and more presentable.

Show me a different way — a together way.

Show me, dear Christ, what it means that you are "gentle"
and "lowly" of heart. For I need gentle and where I am is lower
than I knew I could be.
Help me, vulnerable Christ, to let you into this place that I
somehow hate and still protect.
May this place of pain be the very place
where you make your home.
I in you. You in me.
Where the lines of where you begin and I end become blurry in
this embrace of love.
Here. Yes, even here.

INTRODUCTION

"Bend but don't break." Any fan of the Philadelphia Eagles football team knows this slogan, as it was the rally cry for the Eagles defense for a decade. Jim Johnson was the defensive coordinator for the Philadelphia Eagles from 1999-2008, and he remains a legend in the city. He was all grit. He was all tough. He led the Eagles for many years with that motto that kept our boys playing hard and usually losing only because of the lack of offense. "Bend but don't break."

It would be nice to say that's how I have gone through my life, but it would also not be true. I would have to settle for a statement that has less bravado and more accuracy: "Sometimes bend. Other times, completely break. Just don't die."

I struggled through high school and college with anxiety and depression. It was the time when I also fell in love with Jesus, but I was barely hanging on. I was bending further than I wanted to admit.

At 21, I graduated college and began a ministry position at a church. It is also the time that I had my first break. I don't have a better word than that. My mind, which had experienced pain before, felt like it simply fractured. Any defense I had against darkness was obliterated, and so was I.

I pursued - not for the first time - Christian counseling to help make sense of this overwhelming internal pain that I was experiencing. I eventually was diagnosed with Obsessive Compulsive Disorder.

Since that time, I have served in the local church and am currently pastoring at a wonderful faith family in New Jersey. Throughout my adult life, I have had several seasons of bends and breaks. At times, this struggle has been a pebble in my shoe. At times, this has been a boulder that I have been crushed underneath. At times, it has been dormant. At other times, I would have given just about anything for it to tire and leave me alone. Often, it has taken the things I loved and turned them into monsters of terror and obsession.

I have, during the darkest of seasons, begged him to take my mental anguish away and he often hasn't. He has allowed it to refine, change and slay me. I have learned it is not because he is cruel or indifferent. If there is anything I know in the throes of mental and emotional suffering is that God weeps with those of us who weep. In the midst of my anguish, there has been much kindness, much relief and many "pools in the desert" (Psalm 84).

I would not change my story if I could, but it is not the one I would have written. I would not have the courage to write it. There are many seasons I have not felt the courage to live it.

Along the way, I have had the chance to walk together with dear friends who share in suffering. Every story is different and no one carries hardship in the exact same way, but I have been able to journey with those who were seeking to discover Christ in the painful path of mental and emotional suffering. The stories have been familiar enough that we are humming the same tune even if we have somewhat different lyrics.

I write this book from a couple of specific vantage points. The first is from my own experience as a frequent sufferer of mental and emotional hardship. The second is from my time as a pastor and a spiritual director, where I have been able to partner with people in many seasons of pain.

In writing this, I have spent my time with a few specific people in mind. I primarily write to a follower of Jesus who knows resilient mental and emotional pain and wonders where God could possibly be in the midst of it. I also hope this could be of service to a loved one of someone who is undergoing a long season of internal suffering, that is both confused by it and doesn't know how to help. Lastly, I write to pastors and ministers of souls that want joy for all, but who must - like Elihu - pull up a chair and sit with sufferers while it is still dark.

I would like to make 4 distinctions before I begin. Walking into a conversation about suffering warrants clarity. Being reckless or unclear with words causes unnecessary pain.

   1. I am speaking to people who recognize that they have mental and emotional pain. They know it because they feel it. We will not spend our time listing all types or causes of such suffering. Mental and emotional pain is

appropriately put into categories such as shame, anxiety, loneliness, effects of trauma, insecurity, depression, grief, spiritual darkness and other interior places of loss and despair. Throughout the history of the church and the world, these have had different labels, but the ailments of the soul have always been with us. My aim here is not to academically catalogue and describe all the types of internal pain. I am also not trying to list every cause or reason for them. Mental and emotional pain are greatly influenced by genetics, external circumstances, physical and mental illnesses and relational ruptures. For our time here, we will look less at the causes of all internal suffering - but how to walk with Christ in the midst of them.

2. This book is not a therapeutic book or any replacement for the need of therapy. My training is in pastoral ministry and in spiritual direction. Spiritual direction does not look wholly unlike counseling but its aim is specifically to help a person find the presence of God in the midst of their need. I am often approached by such people in ministry and work in conjunction with local Christian therapists and psychiatrists. The need for these other professionals is paramount and the spiritual direction that I do is often in concert with their work, not intended to be a replacement of it.

3. I don't primarily write to explain the mystery of "why does God allow bad things to happen to good people?" There are theologians who have wrestled with that for

centuries and have done great work at doing so, most of them thoughtfully concluding that there are no simple answers to this question. I can say that at the end of the day, so many of us who have suffered have landed in the firm conviction that God is indeed good and near, but the mechanics of why he does what he does and why he allows what he allows are less known to us. Here, I am less focused on the broad theological question of "why" and more focused on the pastoral question of "how." How do we then live when our Christ allows great suffering in our lives? But, even more specifically, how can we know and enjoy the love and presence of God amidst the mental and emotional pain?

4. I will speak of my own story, which includes struggles with depression and anxiety. A lot of that struggle is linked to Obsessive Compulsive Disorder, that has been a weight for me to carry for most of my life. However, this is not to assume that everyone who has a mental disorder suffers the same mental anguish as I do. Some suffer less. Some suffer more. There are also those who suffer emotionally and mentally who do not have a mental disorder. So, while my story includes my illness, I have found the pilgrims that I most closely identify with are those who know chronic or semi-chronic interior pain and struggle regardless of diagnosis or reason. This is not a book about mental illness. It is a book about mental and emotional darkness that visits those of us with labels and those of us without.

1

GOD'S GLORY AND THE SUFFERING SOUL

In John 17, we have the longest prayer of Christ recorded in Scripture. He prays this on Thursday of Passion Week before receiving the cross. Jesus' prayer details the reason for his mission on earth. It is his final cry to the Father before the ultimate war was waged and won over that weekend. I believe it is the clearest explanation in Scripture of why the Godhead created and redeemed creation. He begins his prayer with how time itself began, with the glory of God.

> When Jesus spoke these words, he lifted up his eyes to heaven and said, Father, the hour has come; glorify your Son that the Son may glorify you, since you have given him authority over all flesh, to give eternal life to all whom you have given him. And this is eternal life, that

they know you, the only true God, and Jesus Christ whom you have sent. I glorified you on earth, having accomplished the work that you gave me to do. And now, Father, glorify me in your own presence with the glory that I had with you before the world existed. (John 17:1-3)

This long story of redemption displays and declares the glory of God. In the kindness of God, we are included in this story and glory giving. We are participants in the "eternal life", which Jesus defined as knowing "the only true God and Jesus Christ whom you have sent" (v. 3).

The Westminster shorter catechism sums it up this way: "Man's chief end is to glorify God and to enjoy him forever."[1]

The glory of God in Christ is crucial in every discussion. In every part of our complicated selves, in every season of our lives, this matters. The Apostle Paul wrote to the people in Corinth, "So, whether you eat or drink, or whatever you do, do all to the glory of God" (1 Corinthians 10:31). Every part. Everything. To God's glory.

But, what about sorrow? What about depression or agony that comes when it feels like our insides are being pounded by an angry chef on a lean piece of meat? What about when people experience loss after loss, compounding grief and loneliness? How does God's glory intersect with those of us who struggle with utter anguish or crippling anxiety? Paul said, "Whether I eat or drink …". Well, Paul, what about when I don't feel that I have the courage to take the next step, the desire to do so and am so confused I don't even know which direction I should go?

Eating and drinking seem like simple enough glory tasks. But where is the glory in this?!

This has been a key question of my life. How can I glorify God and find his true joy in the midst of struggling with seasons of devastating mental and emotional pain?

Seeking to understand God's glory in this is not simple. But, we wish it were. We want quick and clear answers to problems. Pain is a problem, and platitudes and quippy answers will not serve those who know its depth and complexity.

Here are some ways that we can oversimplify the response to mental and emotional suffering in the church of Christ. They are each well intended messages that are given to people all over the world who are in the throes of struggle. There are very few of us who have not faced some version of each of these oversimplifications by well-meaning Christians. They are exaggerated here but are the root system of a lot of advice given to hurting people.

Oversimplification 1:

It is God's glory that we dismiss or downplay mental and emotional anguish.

The thought goes like this:

The Lord is good and gives good things. Suffering does not seem very good and so if it is happening, God's glory is not involved and we should stop experiencing it. People are made for joy in the Lord, so someone who deals with bouts of intense darkness needs to snap out of it and be grateful that they are redeemed and headed for Heaven. It's going to be okay!

The people I have heard espouse a position like this tend to have a strong view of Scripture. However, I do not think it is a thorough view of Scripture, but a convenient one that does not have a lot of room for the people who wrote and populated its pages.

The Bible speaks constantly about suffering. Jesus demonstrates and teaches how we are to approach suffering. When Jesus approached suffering, his response was not and is not now dismissal, or with statements like "Chin up! You're going to be okay." It's one of my favorite things about him.

He chooses not to dismiss but to engage. Dane Ortlund writes,

> The cumulative testimony of the four Gospels is that when Jesus Christ sees the falseness of the world all about him, his deepest impulse, his most natural instinct, is to move toward that sin and suffering, not away from it.[2]

Oversimplification 2:

It is God's glory that we exorcise the spiritual darkness that is mental and emotional suffering.

The thought goes like this:

Call the oldest priest in town and tell him to bring his biggest crucifix and let's do this thing.

Demons are real and are present in our world. Spiritual darkness can and does present at times as lasting despair. However, to quickly categorize interior pain as the dominion of hell is to both give too much credit to spiritual darkness and potentially dangerous solutions for finding hope. This also loudly communicates that God surely is not involved in this type of suffering. This must be only from hell. This view robs Heaven of some of its greatest lessons and seasons of growth and dismisses a God wise and kind enough to even use sorrow for good.

Oversimplification 3:

It is for God's glory that we overcome all mental anguish.

The thought goes like this:

This type of suffering is real and substantive and it gets in the way of God's glory. It keeps us from efficiently serving others, operating in the world and distracts us from volunteering in the nursery or stacking chairs at church. It is an obstacle that is meant to be conquered through confession, prayer and grit. You know, if you just try a little harder, read a few more great books, pray this magic prayer enough, you will find health and deliverance.

This thought process is understandable for people who love God and do not understand what living with interior pain is truly like. 1st Thessalonians speaks so clearly about how we are to approach the different ailments of the human condition.

> And we urge you, brothers, admonish the idle, encourage the fainthearted, help the weak, be patient with them all. (1 Thessalonians 5:14)

We do great harm if we use the wrong tool when dealing with people. To admonish the faint hearted as if they were simply living in idleness can cause spiritual abuse and deep damage to someone who may be earnestly seeking God but is still struggling with mental and emotional pain. Great harm has been done by well meaning, oversimplifying people.

Oversimplification 4:

It is for God's glory that we avoid dealing with this lest we do harm by our ignorance.

The thought goes like this:

This is a question for a psychologist. This type of pain and confusion is too defended by our quick counsel and Bible verses. Let God deal with the people who have normal insides; a person suffering like this should go to a professional who can handle them. If and when they can return to a typical baseline, they are ready for the real Christian life.

Some individuals and churches wisely understand that they are ill-equipped to deal with anxiety, depression, loneliness, insecurity, grief or sorrow. They are not trained (nor should they have to be) to understand the layers of complexity that weave through many of life's difficult situations.

However, at times, we can punt and send people to psychologists and counselors, when they also need spiritual growth and development. Both psychology and medication have accomplished wonderful things in people's lives. They have in mine. By themselves, however, medication or psychoanalysis do not help someone learn and receive the love of God. If the Gospel does not apply to those who are under resilient darkness, then the Gospel is not for everyone.

The way out of oversimplifying God's glory in suffering is not to read a book. It is experiencing suffering for yourself or loving someone who is going through the confusion of it. It is only when our preconceived notion of how we thought God would behave is struck down, that we need to seek more understanding. True Christian love is always the best teacher and loving a sufferer, whether that be ourselves or another, leads to a knowing that is deeper than words are able to take us.

Having said that, here are some attempts to speak to how God's glory intersects with the complicated dark.

1. There is no inherent glory in suffering.

We were not designed to be in pain. God, in his good and intended creation, made us like him in his image (Genesis 1:26).

We are wonderfully and fearfully made (Psalm 139:14) and are designed to watch over God's created order here on earth (Psalm 8). Our minds are a fascinating and beautiful reflection of our creator. Our hearts are a beautiful display of his affections. We reflect his imagination, delight, governance, organization, compassion, care, relational capacity, creative insight and an ability to function out of love for him, others and ourselves.

God design is "good." It is Shalom. It is all things working together in concerted wholeness.

He did not design humans to operate with mental and emotional anguish. This is not to criticize those who experience this anymore than those who struggle with a food allergy. Our interior world was designed to be whole and will return to that design. Every one of us have features of neurosis, over obsession, anxiety, grief, disconnection in relating to others, and feelings of unexplained despair. Our minds are dealing with the post-fallen world. Some of us deal with that to a deeper level than others. Praise God, that is not the way we were designed to be.

 Beth Moore, in her memoir, details her relationship with her husband, Keith. She wrote, with Keith's permission, about his struggle with inner pain due to childhood trauma. Beth, who does not struggle in the same way that Keith does, writes about their interaction.

> He told me once, "Lizabeth, life is harder for some people than others. I wanted to argue with him. I wanted to say how everyone had the same opportunity to be happy in Jesus. I wanted to ask him why the blessings of the present couldn't make up for the curses of the past... Life is harder for some people than others. Shadows follow me often enough, but not incessantly. Not everywhere I go... I deal with bouts of anxiety and depression, but they don't chase me down constantly like ravenous wolves after a bleeding sheep.... Two wounds could cause the same amount of stitches and yet cause varied levels of pain.[3]

 To both of their courage and credit, they admit something that those in anguish already know. Sometimes things are not right. Sometimes, it is more unbearable for some than others. It is what it is, but what it is feels broken and inflamed. Never should we tell a sufferer the trite response that this is how life was intended to be felt and lived.[4] Jesus conducted 39 recorded miracles in the New Testament. There is not one miracle where

Jesus took someone from wellness to fracture; from thriving to pain. Legs were made to run. Eyes were made to see. The interior life was made for communion, order, service and joy.

One of the darkest moments of my life was the day I received my greatest affirmation. My grandfather, who did not dole out praise often, took me aside when I was 16 years old. He spoke to me about how proud that he was of me and that he saw me truly becoming a man of God. It was a sacred moment from grandfather to son, almost like he was speaking to me as a rite of passage on my spiritual journey. It carried a lot of weight for both of us. I remember where I was on the navy blue couch in my living room as he shared these kind and weighty words.

I left that conversation, went upstairs to a small corner of the house and wept in utter hopelessness. He, along with several other important people in my life, were deeply affirming that I was living the Christian life just as it was meant to be lived.

The problem was that I was completely haunted and broken. Openly so. I had an undiagnosed mental illness that left me battling with fear and depression. I knew that even though I was operating in the world in a way that made my grandfather proud, there was something wrong. I was not designed to function like this. Please, God, let me not function like this. Let this not be the design.

To tell those of us who have seasons of intense mental and emotional pain that this is how a benevolent God made us to function speaks directly to us that he is not a benevolent God.

I had a good friend talk to me once about how many people in his life had gone through seasons of dark depression. He admitted that he was a little jealous of the lessons they learned and he wished he could understand the experience and have a go at it himself.

You could have scraped my jaw off the floor with a pancake flipper.

Why would anyone ever want to do that?! Only someone who has no clue how dark depression is would ever say such a thing. We do not need to glorify suffering as a badge of honor. We do not need to defend it as if God has joy when his people are under its crushing weight. It is not special or noble to experience pain. The pain itself is not the glory of God or the glory of the person experiencing it.

Yes, our Savior does not rescue us from all suffering.

Yes, God uses suffering in the life of the pilgrim to accomplish things that could only be done by fire.

Yes, he does not allow great harm without having great healing in mind.

This does not mean that we should wish for, or undergo one minute of suffering as if it were the only healthy choice of the faith follower. When it is God's will that we live in fullness and peace, that is only a wonderful thing. When it's his will that we suffer, it can produce a wonderful thing. But the forever design in the kingdom is all wholeness and joy.

2. God is deeply glorified by drawing near to people with mental and emotional anguish.

There are not many truths that I believe more than this. While there is no inherent specialness or glory to suffering, it is a tool that God uses and even a burden that he assigns to accomplish something special; something truly holy. Thus, while suffering should never be chosen for suffering's sake, when the good God allows it for a time, He has a purpose and will accomplish something wholly good.

If you had a slippery Bible and words could fall off the pages, and you gave it a good shake, you would have a couple of giant piles of words about suffering. One of those piles would be about how God relieves and rescues his people from suffering. The other pile would be how God acts as a companion to those who remain in it. Let's start with how God comes alongside.

In Psalm 23, David writes,

> Even though I walk through the valley of the shadow of death, you are with me. Your rod and your staff comfort me. (Psalms 23:4)

In Psalm 84 and other places, David - who was nomadic for several years in the desert and caves of Israel - speaks candidly about traveling through mental and spiritual valleys of death. It's not fun. Valleys of death always feel like valleys of death. Yet, this is the miracle that can be found in the darkness of the torment: He is still there.

I remember when I first wrestled with very dark depression as a result of my OCD. It felt as if 90% of my mind was screaming in pain and accusation and 10% was trying to navigate the world, operate in ministry and function like a person.

I cried out to God through journaling. My desperate plea was, "Please don't let me keep falling." I had this image in my mind of me literally falling into a pit of darkness. Each morning, I hoped I would reach bottom. Each morning, I wondered if I had. *Please, dear God, let this be the worst of it and bring me back.* I would pray to Jesus, "But not my will but yours be done." Eventually, those prayers and journal entries stopped attempting to exhibit the nobility of Christ, and I dropped the "I will go through this if you want me to" type of prayers.

I simply plead. *Please, no further down. Please, no further darkness.* Many of my journal entries simply had the word 'please' repeated over and over on the page. I remember starting to wake up and run in the early mornings to try to pound my electrocuted mind into the pavement. I ran harder and faster than I ever had. I lived in Chicago then and I had hope each time I would pass an alley. My fantasy was that I would go by one of those alleys and a speeding car would be timed perfectly to kill me on the spot.

God ended this season of suffering in the next years that followed. He provided great relief to my soul. He did so after letting me fall past where I knew and mind and soul could survive. He let me fall and keep falling past where I could see light anymore. What he showed me is a lesson that I will never forget. He showed me that he is present in the dark, too. I desperately was looking for light at the top of the hole I was falling in. What I found was not light but a companionship in the dark. This remains the greatest apologetic that I have for my Savior in my life.

This next thing I write is not something that I have shared with many people. It was during a more recent spike in anxiety. I went and took a retreat with the Lord to listen to him. I have a place I go to in New Jersey - yes, God lives even in New Jersey - where he has met me many times. I went there to listen for a couple of days to see if God had anything to say to me as our church was heading into a transition and my wife and I were readying for a surprise 4th child.

I heard him ask me a question as I walked with him on the familiar trail that we take:

What do you want?

This took me by complete surprise. He has never asked me that before. I actually don't remember God ever asking me anything. I am usually the one doing the asking and he is the one doing the rescuing, providing, assuring. But not this day.

My first reaction was, "woah, is this really a Solomon type moment where I get one wish?" I have long preached that God is not a genie, and here he was asking me this question. I discredited the voice that I heard because it did not sound like something God would say. Yet, he was not as impressed at my theological shake down and the question remained.

What do you want from Me?

My second reaction was, "What should I want?" I thought of the salvation of all of my children. I thought of the rescue or cure for my OCD. I thought of financial security for my family. Then I thought of Solomon and what he asked for. He asked for wisdom to lead and govern God's people. Our church was at a time of transition where our founding and senior pastor was retiring after 40 years. Surely, the people I serve could use a Solomon type of selfless request.

But, through these two reactions was the deep pull of my soul.

It was the honest thing I wanted. It was the thing that I have known to be the most special and precious thing of my life. It was deeper than the noble or selfless wants. It wasn't a super spiritual one, but one that came from the youngest and most honest part of myself. It was stronger than the wants I have as a parent or a pastor. It was the guttural want of my life.

I want to be with you. I want to be with you and feel your presence for my whole life. I will go wherever you lead me, and I sure would like more green pastures than death valleys. But, more than that, I just want to do whatever we do together.

I shared this with a dear friend and pastor and he told me, mostly kidding, "You wasted it! God already promised that! You should have asked for something else!" But when God asked, this was my heart's desire. Not because I had become holy or chosen all the right ways to handle suffering. But, because after going through seasons of mental and emotional savagery, I knew he was what my soul was made for.

This is what suffering has taught me:

1. It is agony to suffer.
2. Even if I cannot see him or directly feel him at times, I   never suffer alone.
3. It is better to fall into the deep and dark with him than it is to live without him.

It is only in the school of suffering that we learn this: he is all we need. God's companionship in the dark is the primary treasure found in the dark. But here, we learn the deep and significant value of that gift. He really is everything.

3. It is God's glory to heal us from mental and emotional anguish and suffering at an appointed and unknown time.

Yes, it is his glory. It is his great delight. Rescuing his people is what makes God himself sing and dance in Zephaniah 3.

Does that mean it will come soon? We don't know. God does not give exact timelines.

Does it mean it will come in this life? We don't know. It usually does but not always.

Regardless of his good (and often long) timing, he delights to heal and restore. Each restoration is a testament of the resurrection of Christ himself. Our forever eternal life will be a lasting and continual celebration of that.

Frederick Buechner writes about his own journey,

> Neurotic anxiety happens to be my own particular demon, a floating sense of doom that has ruined many of what could have been, should have been, the happiest days of my life, and more than a few times in my life I have been raised from such ruins, which is another way of saying that more than a few times in my life I have been raised from death - death of the spirit anyway, death of the heart - by the healing power that Jesus calls us both to heal with and to be healed by.[5]

David talked about the action of waiting on God "more than watchmen wait for the morning" (Psalm 130:6). I am not a watchman but I have done a few all nighters when I was a youth director at a church. The nights are long when you can't sleep through them. Dealing with tired teenagers seems really impossible after midnight. It feels dark at 1am, but somehow even looks darker at 2am or 3am etc.

The waiting for dawn to break is an active one, not a passive one. It is not just sitting back and seeing when the day will come. It is waiting for it. It is holding on to hope that feels painful to hold on to because of the daunting question, "What if it never shows?" Dawn is not something that we feel can happen "at some time". It is something that we need to see as soon as possible.

We find comfort that Christ will not delay a second longer than he should. He will not only wait with us, he delights with all of heaven's wonder to come and rescue us when it is time.

Prayer of the afflicted:

Father, rescue me from the pit;
This horrible, hungry monster of darkness.
Give me help because right now, my felt need seems
bigger than any spiritual one I can come up with.
Even as I come to you wanting your glory, I want it barely.

Because barely is all that I have right now.

Please.
Please make your presence known.
Companion with me here in the dark.
Take me eventually to the light.
See me through.
I ask this suffering would be only as long as absolutely
necessary, and I pray that from it, I would know a little more
that you are everything I need.

---

[1] This is the answer to the 1st of 107 questions in *The Shorter Catechism with Scripture Proofs; The Westminster Assembly* (New Zealand: Titus Books, 2014)

[2] Ortlund, Dane. *Gentle and Lowly: The Heart of Christ for Saints and Sinners* (Wheaton, IL: Crossway, 2020).

[3] Moore, Beth. *All my Knotted-Up Life: A Memoir* (Carol Stream, IL: Tyndale 2023).

[4] I want to make a quick interjection. What many people did with the story of Keith and Beth Moore, was ask themselves a question: *"where does my life rank on the 'harder' scale'"*? My fear here is that anyone would read these words or the words of my own story and say, "well, I don't have it so bad. My pain or suffering is not that valid." Comparing pain never works because it always leaves us feeling bad for ourselves: we feel we have more pain or feel like our pain doesn't count if we feel we have less.

Each person's pain matters and none of us truly knows where our story ranks on the human suffering scale. Please know that wherever you are, you matter and your story matters. Deeply. When we are talking about mental and emotional pain, there are not clean categories types, causes or amount of pain that can be notched on a linear scale.

[5] Buechner, Frederick. *Secrets in the Dark; A Life in Sermons.* (New York, NY: Harper Collins, 2006).

2

SUFFERING AND SPIRITUAL FORMATION

I had come to Michigan to meet with my grandfather's psychiatrist. Anxiety and depression run deep through my mom's side of the family. The psychiatrist was familiar with our family and had agreed to meet with me.

Before this, I met with a counseling pastor in Chicago, where I was doing youth ministry. After a few meetings with me, he told me - to his credit - that I was out of his league, and I needed to find a professional to help explain the confusion and darkness I was in. He was a dear man and said it to me kindly in his church office. But what I heard was not dissimilar to one of my favorite Farside Comic strips. In the comic, a man lies on the couch talking about his problems, while a counselor writes his case notes. There are only three words that the counselor has sketched on his notepad: "Just plain nuts!".[6] That is what it felt

to me as I walked down Milwaukee Avenue on the 2 mile walk
in Chicago back to my apartment.

I didn't know where to go, but my grandfather had been
haunted most of his life by anxiety, so I thought I would check
in with him. He was, along with others in his family before and
after him, a struggler. He was the Chairperson of the Science
Department of Taylor University and founder of Au Sable, a
Christian Environmentalist Camp in Mancelona, MI. His
brother, who struggled every bit as he did and details his
journey in his book, *On a Hill Far Away*[7], was a missionary
surgeon and started a missions agency in Rwanda. Interior
agony does not discriminate.

I was 15 minutes into a meeting with this psychiatrist when he
changed my understanding of discipleship and redirected the
rest of my life. I have no way of knowing if this man knew or
cared about Jesus. He knew that I did and was able to speak a
targeted wisdom to me that no preacher or Christian counselor
had before him.

He gave me a diagnosis, and I basically begged him to say it
was not true. My plea was not dissimilar from a doctor looking
at an X-ray of a broken arm of an athlete and the patient
begging, "Can you look one more time to make sure? Maybe
it's a cream cheese smudge on the printout."

He said this to me. "Ben, this is your cross that Jesus is asking
you to carry. It is your choice to carry it or not. But, this is your
cross." The words are decades old at this point, but I can hear
them as if they were spoken this morning.

In a few words, he helped me understand that this suffering I was experiencing was something not to just be avoided. It was something to be stewarded. It was not an impediment to my spiritual formation. It was a messy, painful, allowed opportunity to know him better. This has helped me through the shame of feeling different than others that I feel have an easier mental experience than I do. If this is a cross, my calling is to carry it - not pretend it doesn't exist or hide it from those I love.

Discipleship is not only about what things we pray for, what verses we memorize and how to love our neighbors. Part of following Jesus is picking up our unique, heavy and painful cross as we follow him. It is the stewarding of our suffering.

Then Jesus said to his disciples, "Whoever wants to be my disciple must deny themselves and take up their cross and follow me. For whoever wants to save their life will lose it, but whoever loses their life for me will find it. What good will it be for someone to gain the whole world, yet forfeit their soul? Or what can anyone give in exchange for their soul? For the Son of Man is going to come in his Father's glory with his angels, and then he will reward each person according to what they have done. (Matthew 16:24-27).

When Jesus talked about a cross, he was speaking of two pieces of wood crafted for death. A cross was used to publicly torture and humiliate criminals in order to demonstrate to others that they should keep in line lest they ever have to experience agony like this.

Jesus says, take up that cross.

I don't like my cross. I never have. In my insensitive moments, I have said to my friends, "Why couldn't I just have some normal struggle like an overwhelming temptation to have a porn addiction." That was cruel and selfish of me to say that, and it didn't land well because that was their cross. It was a crushing weight they had to carry as they daily tried to live sober. The reality is that no one wants a cross. No one likes their cross. A cross is not designed to be enjoyed. It is designed to be endured daily.

I can see some hairs on some theology necks rising. "But Jesus endured the cross, so we don't have to." Yes, this is true - forever, eternal, life-altering true! Jesus took the cross that bore our penalty of sin and the power of it over our daily lives. But the cross he bore did not eliminate our suffering.

Spurgeon writes in Morning by Morning in 1865,

> Mark then, Christian, Jesus does not suffer so as to exclude your suffering. He bears a cross, not that you may escape it, but that you may endure it. Christ exempts you from sin, but not from sorrow. Remember that, and expect to suffer.[8]

Jesus wants his followers to not be unaware. Suffering of many types would come their way. The bearing of suffering and the formation in Christ within it defines much of the Christian journey. Learning to bear the crosses that we have is the cost of discipleship.

In Matthew 16, Jesus gives us the reason to learn to bear our cross. He does not call us to take up our cross out of blind obedience. He does so, making sure that we know that what we gain is far more than what we lose.

> For whoever wants to save their life will lose it, but

whoever loses their life for me will find it. (v. 25)

It is in the loss of our addiction to the self life and the acceptance of the cross of discipleship that we find that life "which is truly life" (1 Timothy 6:19). Cross-bearers have sung, testified and wept over this beautiful truth throughout the world and throughout time. Truly, what we carry is much smaller than what we gain.

Yet, even though we gain much, it does not diminish the severity of what we carry.

The question is, are we willing to bear it?

On that day in the psychiatrist's office, he helped me see that this cross was painful and potentially permanent for my life on earth. Whether he knew it or not, he also gave me my first step on how to honor and deal with this suffering. I am invited to carry it in obedience for as long as it is assigned.

Warren Wiersbe wrote a book titled, *Why Us? When Bad Things Happen to God's People.* He recalls a story of a ministry encounter he had with a dear friend.

> Her husband had gone blind and then had come down with an incurable disease. She had a slight stroke that forced her to retire from her secretarial job and become a full-time "seeing-eye wife." Although they had many friends, they had no children.
>
> Attempting to encourage her one day, I said, "I want you to know that we're praying for you."
>
> "I appreciate that," she replied. "What are you praying for God to do?"
>
> As she waited for my reply, I found myself struggling

for a mature answer. I had never really been confronted with the question before! After all, when people are suffering, you pray for healing (if it's God's will), for strength, for special mercy in pain, and so on, and this is what I told her.

"Thank you," she said, "but please pray for one more request. Pray that I won't waste all of this suffering."[9]

What a beautiful request.

As we deal with people, we need utter compassion and gentleness in the midst of suffering. We also need the kindness of calling people to bear their crosses with fidelity to Christ lest the suffering be wasted.

In writing my own Rule of Life, I include the various resources of my life and seek to learn and serve Christ with them. These include my money, relationships, time, body, life calling and possessions. This also includes the stewardship of my cross. In my Rule of Life, I put it this way,

> As a part of the design of my life, I am assigned a cross. This cross is a wretched tree on which the ego and the flesh are crucified. This cross is meant to be accepted and carried daily. The moment I lose sight of my calling to walk step-by-step with my cross is the moment that I stop learning from Christ in it and am most susceptible to be crushed underneath of it.[10]

One of the great allegorical works ever penned about God's companionship is *Hinds' Feet in High Places*. It was written by Hannah Hurnard, a missionary to both Palestine and Israel for 50 years. The allegory is a beautiful and tough read. In the story, the main character, Much Afraid, travels from the Kingdom of Fear to the Kingdom of Love. Along the way, she has dear conversations with the loving Chief Shepherd who represents Jesus. In one scene, the Chief Shepherd gives two companions to walk with her. She is giddy at the thought of not traveling alone. The Chief Shepherd presents her companions, saying, "They are good teachers; indeed, I have few better.... This," said he, motioning to the first of the silent figures, "is Sorrow. And the other is her sister, Suffering".[11]

Much Afraid is terrified and heartbroken that these would be her travel buddies and that they would be part of what guided her to the Kingdom of Love. The story continues on her journey until she arrives. It is not only she who is forever changed, but the companions as well. Along the confusing way, they were just what she needed.

Didn't we say that there is no inherent glory in suffering?! Why would Jesus assign suffering if there is not inherent glory in it? Dear reader, hear this. It is because there is great glory in the union of Christ that can be accomplished through it. Does he glory in the pain? No. Is his glory on full display with what he does within these seasons of hardship? Yes!

How do we bear the cross of mental and emotional suffering?

1.Identify it.

Calvin begins his Institutes of the Christian Religion by saying,

> Nearly all the wisdom we possess, that is to say, true and sound wisdom, consists of two parts: the knowledge of

God and of ourselves. But, while joined by many bonds, which one precedes and brings from the other is not easy to discern.[12]

The intricate journey of knowing our inner selves is vital for those who want to bear their cross in the way that Jesus asks. We cannot follow the calling of Christ or know him very well if we do not put in that work. And it is work.

Everyone has a different cross. For many, their specific burdens and crosses change over time. Some people carry a cross from conversion to eternal graduation. Many crosses are a bit easier to carry and some are absolutely crushing. It is important to be able to articulate what you are called to carry, for it is tough to know how to carry what you don't understand. Recently, at our church, we took a group of new leaders through the process of identifying a cross that Christ has called them to bear. It was painful and beautiful to hear the stories and unique burdens. It was evident how Christ had used those brutal sticks of death to bring about deep resurrection and a relationship with him.

If you have trouble knowing how to identify your cross, begin by asking the same thing a physician would, "Where does it hurt?" Surely, not all pain is a cross and much of the pain that you and I experience is a consequence of our actions and is a self-inflicted/infected wound. Those hurts are a calling for you to change. But if you identify a place where things are painful or weighty and you are not given the help to change it, then - for this time - this is your cross.

2. Experience it.

The temptation of every human who undergoes hardship is to ask, "Who is to blame for this?" and "How can I get out of it as soon as possible?" It is no wonder that bitterness and distraction are chief temptations for those going through difficult times.

One of the most common ways to avoid cross-bearing is to try our best to inoculate ourselves from experiencing it. We are in an age where we have access to constant information and entertainment. Many people will not have a quiet moment from the time that they wake up and check their email on their phone until they fall asleep to the TV at night. In every room of the house, every space at the workplace, there is constant opportunity to be distracted by "amusing ourselves to death"[13]. None of us believe this makes us happy, but we all know that it can serve to avoid what makes us really sad or empty. We live in an easy age to not feel anything coming from within ourselves because we are constantly absorbing from the outside. Our mental anguish can get buried. We know it's there. We spend a lot of time managing it, but to let it surface sounds terrifying.

Cross-bearers of internal suffering are brave folk. They are willing to admit with knocking knees that they are not well and what they are experiencing is really difficult. They fearfully are willing to open the door to that closet because they know if they don't, Christ will never occupy that space. They honestly admit that they are not okay and they need help. This is a testimony to their God, who does not need them to be happy if they are not and who can hold their truth, whatever it may be. Sometimes, we try so hard to paint silver linings on storm clouds and call it brave. It isn't. Entering the storm is.

Henri Nouwen put it this way,

> How can we embrace poverty as a way to God when
> everyone around us wants to become rich? Poverty has
> many forms. We have to ask ourselves: 'What is my
> poverty?' Is it lack of money, lack of emotional stability,
> lack of a loving partner, lack of security, lack of safety,
> lack of self-confidence? Each human being has a place
> of poverty. That's the place where God wants to dwell!
> 'How blessed are the poor,' Jesus says (Matthew 5:3).
> This means that our blessing is hidden in our poverty.
>
> We are so inclined to cover up our poverty and ignore it
> that we often miss the opportunity to discover God, who
> dwells in it. Let's dare to see our poverty as the land
> where our treasure is hidden.[14]

We often know so little of both light and dark because we are not willing to experience our poverty. Our senses are dulled to see everything in dim shades. This world has so much beauty and so much sorrow. Brave cross-bearers are given the gift of experiencing both, becoming like him in his unmuted death and becoming like him in his glorious resurrection.

3. Use suffering as a way of knowing and identifying with Christ

> … that I may know him and the power of his
> resurrection, and may share his sufferings, becoming
> like him in his death, that by any means possible I may
> attain the resurrection from the dead. (Philippians

3:10-11)

Each time we suffer, we have an opportunity to connect our experience to the Suffering Servant, the "man of sorrows acquainted with grief" (Isaiah 53:3). When a loved one passes, we can experience Christ's loss of John the Baptist, his dear friend (Mark 14:1-13). When dealing with the grief of estranged children, we can recount Christ's words and tears after the entry into Jerusalem.

> O Jerusalem, Jerusalem, the city that kills the prophets and stones those who are sent to it! How often would I have gathered your children together as a hen gathers her brood under her wings, and you were not willing! (Luke 23:37).

Recently, I read this passage in the Gospel of Matthew.

> Now, Jesus was going up to Jerusalem. On the way, he took the Twelve aside and said to them, "We are going up to Jerusalem, and the Son of Man will be delivered over to the chief priests and the teachers of the law. They will condemn him to death and will hand him over to the Gentiles to be mocked and, flogged and crucified. On the third day, he will be raised to life!" (Matthew 20:17-19)

My wife and I talked about how lonely this must have felt for Jesus, the man. He is experiencing a dread that we cannot imagine. This is mental and emotional suffering. He knows that it is time to start the ride towards his own torture and death. He speaks to his closest friends and shares the exact nature of what is going to happen. Not only does no one respond in the text, but by what happens in a few days, it becomes clear that no one truly listened or believed what he was saying. For Christ, that must have been such a lonely and difficult moment. Instead of those closest to him asking him questions, or seeking how they could comfort, the disciples began a debate about who gets to have the most honored place next to Christ in the kingdom. Oof.

I have also felt, in small measure, what it is like to be alone in my experience and to try to share it, only to be received with blank stares. It hurts. It is alienating and it feels like I can't be known.

During these seasons of alienation, we can look into these texts and we can picture him there. We can meditate and ask him, what did this feel like? We can have compassion and identify with his experience just as he has with us. It is a union of soul, knit by shared sorrow. It is using the suffering not to isolate from Jesus, but to join, understand and know him better.

This cross-bearing passage in Matthew 16 must be linked to another teaching of Jesus. This one is easier to digest. It is one that we like to quote more often. At first, these passages look like they are saying something opposite. However, they are saying something deeply complimentary.

Jesus says,

> Come to me, all who labor and are heavy laden, and I will give you rest. Take my yoke upon you, and learn from me, for I am gentle and lowly in heart, and you will find rest for your souls. For my yoke is easy, and my burden is light. (Matthew 11:28-30)

Here, we learn a beautiful truth about what it means to carry a cross. We carry our cross yoked with Christ. A yoke is a shared burden meant for two oxen to be joined together to carry a load. Christ carries our load with us. Sometimes it feels so light and joyful it is as if he is doing all the work. There are other times, where it feels like he is asking us to bear more than we are able. Yet, the cross we bear is always made more light, more restful and more fruitful by the union we have with him. And while we often "labor to enter that rest" (Hebrews 4:11), cross bearers who know weariness and heavy lifting will find rest because of who carries it with them.

4. Find the right people to carry it with.

Paul writes to the Ephesian church,

> I, therefore, a prisoner for the Lord, urge you to walk in a manner worthy of the calling to which you have been called, with all humility and gentleness, with patience, bearing with one another in love, eager to maintain the unity of the Spirit in the bond of peace. (Ephesians 4:1-3)

I have many friends who have kindly cared for me in my journey. One of my friends, who loves me very much, was listening to me talk about the confusion and anxiety I experienced. It was a bit foreign to him and he tried to stick with me one day as I shared what I was struggling through. He didn't last very long.

He said, "Ben, talking to you reminds me of the movie Shrek. I'm Shrek and you're the donkey." If you haven't seen the movie, let me spoil it for you so you can empathize with me.

Shrek is the hero who is strong, bold, a little grumpy, but a good ogre who is at peace with himself and the world. The donkey is annoying, neurotic, constantly talking, and imagining things going wrong. It was not a nice feeling to receive this, perhaps true, but compassionless comparison... I learned he was not the best person to carry those things with.

But, I have also found that through being willing to share and be hurt or misunderstood, there are dear people who will journey with me and I am with them. There are people who love enough to listen, even to the donkeys.

I have the privilege of having a spouse, dear friends and family who do not share my OCD but share in the sufferings of Christ in their own way. With my struggle, they are curious and kind. They ask questions and don't pretend to know or propose to supply the answers. They sit with me, grieve with me and pray for me as I reach out when I need them. The pastors that I pastor with all know this journey of my life and travel with me in it. People like this are hard and necessary to find. People who know pain and sorrow and have found Jesus usually have the most room for this.

James Davison Hunter wrote a book called *To Change the World*.[15] He spends a great deal of time wrestling with how Christians can change the world (if you didn't catch that in the title). His conclusion is that the greatest way to effect change is by "Faithful Presence." I can testify that it is how my world has been changed for the good by those who bear the name of Christ. A non-anxious presence in the face of sorrow is a gift that is truly other.

These relationships do not come easy. I wish that they did. We also have trouble trusting another with our pain because we know what it's like to have that trust mistreated. It is worth the risk to try again. This is simply because we are relationally constructed. You are not made an island. You do not have to be alone. We will talk more about this in chapter 7.

5. Only carry it for today.

Luke records the words of Jesus about cross bearing in his Gospel. He writes,

> And he said to all, "If anyone would come after me, let him deny himself and take up his cross daily and follow me." (Luke 9:23)

What wisdom this is from Christ! We cannot carry tomorrow's cross, especially when the cross we carry is heavy. To add tomorrow's burdens to today is an unnecessary and impossible task. Jesus only asks us to stay present with our cross today. This echoes what Jesus said in the sermon on the Mount:

> Therefore, do not be anxious about tomorrow, for tomorrow will be anxious for itself. Sufficient for the day is its own trouble. (Matthew 6:34)

Alan Noble wrote a book titled On *Getting Out of Bed*; *The Burden and Gift of Living*[16]. He gets his title from the haunting Cormac McCarthy novel, *The Road*, that has the famous quote,

> "What's the bravest thing you ever did?" He spat in the road a bloody phlegm, "getting up this morning", he said.[17]

Noble talks about the burden of daily living.

Despite the comforts of contemporary life and its promises of even greater peace and self-mastery, life is terribly hard. A comfortable, pleasant life isn't normal. And while we may hesitate to call getting out of bed "courageous", it is undeniably true that day-to-day life demands a great deal of courage.[18]

We cannot get out of bed for tomorrow; only today. The practice of not looking to tomorrow's potential weight is a very difficult practice. When today feels bad, tomorrow sounds worse. But, tomorrow's cross is unknown to us yet. Christ has not assigned us tomorrow's cross. The chances are it might look very similar to today, but it is neither for us to know or carry until we get there.

Crosses are brutal, messy instruments of death. When our cross is enduring mental and emotional peril, we need help. That help comes in inches and often only lasts minutes. The crucified Christ is here to help us because he knows how to bear and ultimately resurrect crosses. He has done it before. He is doing it all the time. Though the road be steep and the weight feels too much, he is enough for this day. He will be there for the next, too.

Serenity Prayer for Cross-bearers

God, grant me the serenity
to accept the things, I cannot change,
the courage to change the things I can,
and the wisdom to know the difference.
Living one day at a time,
enjoying one moment at a time;
accepting hardship as a pathway to peace;
taking, as Jesus did,
this sinful world as it is,
not as I would have it;
trusting that You will make all things right
if I surrender to Your will;
so that I may be reasonably happy in this life
and supremely happy with You forever in the next. Amen.[19]

---

[6] Larson, Gary. *Far Side Comic. "Just Plain Nuts."* (Seattle, WA: FarWorks, Inc, March 13, 1990).

[7] Snyder, Albert C. *On a Hill Far Away; Journal of a Missionary Doctor in Rwanda.* (Minneapolis, MN: Light and Life Publishing, 1999)

[8] Spurgeon, Charles. *Morning by Morning; or, Daily Readings For The Family of the Closet.* (New York: Robert Carter and Brothers, 1865).

[9] Wiersbe, Warren. *Why Us? When Bad Things Happen to God's People.* (Grand Rapids, MI: Fleming H. Revell Company, 1984). *Italics his.*

[10] The concept of a *Rule of Life* may sound foreign to some. It is an ancient practice that monastic communities developed. Perhaps the best known of them is from St. Benedict in the 6th century. For those who struggle with mental and emotional pain and confusion, developing a personal *Rule of Life* can provide significant mooring. It serves like the instruments of an airplane when the weather has made it too difficult to know how to navigate by sight. It gives a plum line and rhythm to life that extends past (or through) the volatile feelings or negative thoughts that exist from season to season.

[11] Hurnard, Hannah. *Hinds' Feet in High Places.* (Blacksburg, VA: Wilder Publications, 2010).

[12] Calvin, John. *Institutes of the Christian Religion.* (Philadelphia: The Westminster Press, 1960.). He first published these in Latin in 1536 and later in French in 1541.

[13] This phrase is borrowed from Neil Postman's work by that title. *Amusing Ourselves to Death. Public Discourse in the Age of Show Business. (City of Westminster, London: Penguin Books, 1985).*

In this salient and incisive book, Postman speaks of his concern of what the entertainment industry can do to the schedule and soul of a person, and from that, the society as a whole.

[14] Nouwen, Henri. Bread for the Journey; A Daybook of Wisdom and Faith. (New York, NY: Harper One, 1997).

[15] Hunter, James Davison. *The Irony, Tragedy and Possibility of Christianity in the Late Modern World.* (Walton Street, Oxford: Oxford University Press, 2010).

[16] Noble, Alan. *On Getting out of Bed; The Burden and Gift of Living.* (Downers Grove: Intervarsity Press, 2023).

[17] McCarthy, Cormac. *The Road.* (New York, NY: Alfred A Knopf, 2006)

[18] Noble, Alan. *On Getting out of Bed; The Burden and Gift of Living.* (Downers Grove: Intervarsity Press, 2023).

[19] *The Serenity Prayer* is commonly attributed to Rienhold Niebuhr. There have been different versions that have been used over the years. This version is the one that is read at Celebrate Recovery meetings each week. This prayer and the community of Celebrate Recovery are wonderful examples of daily cross bearing. https://www.celebraterecovery.com/resources/serenity-prayer

3

FELLOWSHIP OF THE TORMENTED IN SCRIPTURE

Peter says in his first letter,

> Humble yourselves, therefore, under the mighty hand of
> God so that at the proper time he may exalt you, casting
> all your anxieties on him, because he cares for you. Be
> sober-minded; be watchful. Your adversary the devil,
> prowls around like a roaring lion, seeking someone to
> devour. Resist him, firm in your faith, knowing that the
> same kinds of suffering are being experienced by your
> brotherhood throughout the world. (1 Peter 5:6–9)

Suffering emotional and mental pain can isolate. It can feel
that no one can truly understand what is going on. Because

attempts to connect with others during pain is a risk that
sometimes is met with more confusion and isolation, the
temptation is to isolate. There are very few of us who think
isolation is a wise decision. But it is not made out of wisdom
but out of weariness and self-preservation. Peter, in his letter,
was so savvy about how to handle the prowling lion of hell;
Satan, in times of darkness, can be such a menace of
discouragement and loneliness.

Peter's admonition is to resist his devouring attempts by
staying firm in the faith. The word faith could be more
accurately understood in our context as the word "trust." We
stand firm in our trust of God, knowing that the same kinds of
suffering are being experienced throughout the world by his
people. He is sustaining them, too.

This chapter is dedicated to some saints who suffered mental
and emotional difficulty in Scripture. The reasons for it and the
way that they handled it were each their own, but they serve as
encouragements to us to simply remind us that we are not alone.

David

The Psalms of David have served millions of sufferers. That is
not a number that I can prove, but I believe it to be on the
conservative end. This is because mental and emotional
suffering is common. This is also because the Scripture has no
better language of the soul than that of David's psalms. David
prays violent and desperate *prayer*s. He trusts in times of doubt.
He trusts God with his anger when he writes Psalms that make
us think, "how did this get into the Bible?" He trusts God with

his disappointment, guilt, sorrow and downright despair.

> How long, O Lord? Will You forget me forever?
> How long will You hide Your face from me?
> How long shall I take counsel in my soul,
> Having sorrow in my heart all the day?
> How long will my enemy be exalted over me?
> Consider and answer me, O Lord my God;
> Enlighten my eyes, or I will sleep the sleep of death.
> Psalm 13:1-3

In Psalm 6, he cries out,
> I am weary with my moaning;
> every night I flood my bed with tears;
> I drench my couch with my weeping.
> My eye wastes away because of grief;
> it grows weak because of all my foes.
> Psalm 6:6-7

In Psalm 69 he says,
> Save me, O God!
> For the waters have come up to my neck.
> I sink in deep mire,
> where there is no foothold;
> I have come into deep waters,
> and the flood sweeps over me.
> I am weary with my crying out;
> my throat is parched.

> My eyes grow dim
> with waiting for my God.
> Psalm 69:1-3

David wrote at least 73 of the Psalms, many of them filled with lament. Lament is an acknowledgement of sorrow and confusion. A few years ago, I felt led to write a lament about a season of ministry. It was incredibly painful. It was much harder than I thought it would be. A lament is an acknowledgement of how hard things are without the balm of trying to say, "Here is why it is good, too!" David's ruthless trust of God meant that he could give God the cries of his heart and trust that God could deal with them without him having to cover for him. Many of the laments end in confessions of deep trust in God's unfailing love and his resolute hope that God would come and rescue. But they are written before David knew when or how God would come. He offered his sorrow and left it at God's feet unresolved. He trusted that God could handle that and come through in his own timing.

In Psalm 139, David gives us a gift. It is a gift of language that can only come from someone who has experienced life's full joy and full sorrow. It is also the reason for the title of this book.

> Where can I go from your Spirit?
> Where can I flee from your presence?
> If I go up to the heavens, you are there;
> if I make my bed in the depths, you are there.
> If I rise on the wings of the dawn,
> if I settle on the far side of the sea,

even there, your hand will guide me,
your right hand will hold me fast.
If I say, "Surely the darkness will hide me
and the light become night around me,"
even the darkness will not be dark to you;
the night will shine like the day,
for darkness is as light to you.
Psalm 139:7-12

How can David make such a proclamation? How can he know that the presence of the Almighty God ranges from the "wings of the dawn" to the "far side of the sea"? How does he know that God can see in the light as well as in the dark? How can he know that God is "even there?"

It is because David went there and found out.

David traveled to each of these realities with an honesty that is detailed in the Psalms. He has gone to the "heavens" and experienced the unfettered goodness of God through great moments, bountiful gifts and joyful presence. He also experienced the guttural moments of both physical and emotional depths. He found out that God is God in the light and God is God in the dark. He details these joys and sorrows in the Psalms. He tells of how God does not just meet us in the possible there, David goes there and says with loud and messy cries, "Yes! Yes, He is even here!" I know of no better starting place for a soul wanting to find language for suffering and fellowship with someone truly knows it.

Hagar and Ishmael

There are some brutal examples of spiritual abuse in Scripture. Hagar is one of the worst.

In Genesis 12 and 15, God came out with his plan of redemption. It would be a new people. That people would start with Abram and Sarai and continue through their family line. The only problem was that it wasn't working. Abram and Sarai want to fulfill the vision God had given them to give birth to a nation, but they couldn't give birth to one child. For decades, God did not deliver on his promise but asked Abram and Sarai to walk in trust.

Sarai hatches a plan out of desperation. Because she is unable to help God and Abram fulfill the promise, she volunteers her servant, Hagar. She tells Abram to go have a baby with her. He does and proves once again that hurting people are often the best at hurting people.

During pregnancy, Hagar was most likely treated with a respect that she had not received in her whole life. She went from background singer to center stage in this story. The problem was that Sarai was having a hard time stepping back from the mic.

Before giving birth to Ishmael, Sarai turns nasty.

> Then Sarai dealt harshly with her [Hagar], and she fled from her. The angel of the Lord found her by a spring of water in the wilderness, the spring on the way to Shur. (Genesis 16:6b-7).

Notice that Hagar didn't run to the arms of God. Why would she? What she knew of the arms of God were from the hands of

Abram and Sarai. They and their God were not safe to run to.

Instead, God pursues her. Their interaction continues in chapter 21.

> And the angel of the Lord said to her, 'Behold, you are pregnant and shall bear a son. You shall call his name Ishmael because the Lord has listened to your affliction.' (Genesis 21:11).

Hagar goes back to Abram and Sarai. Before she does, she gives God a name using words that come from one who has experienced his presence in pain.

> So she called the name of the of the Lord who spoke to her, "You are a God of seeing," for she said, "Truly I have seen him who looks after me." (Genesis 16:3)

After Hagar gave birth to Ishmael, who she believed will be the heir of the new nation, the child begins to grow. The eyes of Abraham's relatives and servants were all affixed to this young child. But now something else happens. God intervenes in Sarah's barrenness and they are able to have a child of their own. This was a great joy to Sarah and Abraham (yes, they got name changes during this time) and they take this blessing and curse the innocent girl and her little boy.

By the time Isaac was weaned, Sarah and Abraham threw Hagar and Ishmael out into the wilderness again (Genesis 21:8-10). They plotted to have a child with her. They made many promises of what it would look like, and then bailed on them all. She was left with only bread and some water.

She finds herself in the desert in utter despair. She is a now a single mom with zero resources or plan of action. She cries out in her anguish.

> When the water in the skin was gone, she put the child under one of the bushes. Then she went and sat down opposite him a good way off, about the distance of a bowshot, for she said, "Let me not look on the death of the child." And as she sat opposite him, she lifted up her voice and wept. (Genesis 21:15-16).

We have discussed in this book mostly mental and emotional suffering. Physical suffering, chronic illness, poverty, and the many ways we can suffer externally have been and are less of a focus, as we have mentioned. But, here, as is often the case, the physical circumstances lead to emotional devastation. It is a reminder that suffering is not easily parsed into categories as one part of our lives always bleeds into the others.

God does not quit on Hagar like his people did. He comes to her and shows himself again, this time not just with promises but with action that backed them up.

The text continues,

> And God heard the voice of the boy, and the angel of God called to Hagar from heaven and said to her, "What troubles you, Hagar? Fear not, for God has heard the voice of the boy where he is." (Genesis 21:17)

God rescues and provides water to save the boy and his mom. In this story, we have language that is so important to one suffering with any affliction.

God is El Roi, "the God of seeing" (Genesis 16). God is the one who has "heard the voice of the boy where he is" (Genesis 21:7). God is not only the God of the Abrahams. God is not only the one who sees and hears and converses with the spiritual or the faith leaders. He came to Hagar in Genesis 16 and to Hagar and Ishmael in Genesis 21 to reiterate a message that decorates the rest of the Scripture. He is near to the broken hearted. He sees. He hears. Are you reading this and feel your story is different? Do you feel that your suffering is too big for even God to handle or too small for him to be trifled with? You may feel that you don't fit into the neat categories of spiritual people.

Remember the story of Hagar. Hagar did not go to God. God came to her. Ishmael did not present himself as anything God needed. He was just a leftover part of the story, discarded by Abraham and Sarah. Yet, God sees. God hears. Your cries matter to him right where you are. You matter to God.

Paul

In my own suffering, I have had to anchor myself in verses and stories in the Bible for survival. As a result, I have had the opportunity to read different books that address this subject from a Christian perspective. There seem to be two stories that frequent this discussion more than the rest. One is the story of Job, and the other is the story of Paul and his "thorn in the flesh" in 2 Corinthians 12. This is for good reason, because each of these stories is so deeply personal and theological. I have chosen not to include Job for time's sake, but that is not because of the import of his story or the grace that is found there for those who struggle.

I do want to look at Paul in 2 Corinthians 12. Paul was a person who knew suffering of all types. Since coming to faith in

Christ, he saw many wonders of God and was used by him to launch the movement of the church. Along the way, he had some rough patches.

In the passage before 2 Corinthians 12, he names them.

> Five times I received at the hands of the Jews the forty lashes less one. Three times I was beaten with rods. Once I was stoned. Three times I was shipwrecked; a night and a day I was adrift at sea; on frequent journeys, in danger from rivers, danger from robbers, danger from my own people, danger from Gentiles, danger in the city, danger in the wilderness, danger at sea, danger from false brothers; in toil and hardship, through many a sleepless night, in hunger and thirst, often without food, in cold and exposure. (2 Corinthians 11:24-27)

Those are some rough circumstances; circumstances that jump off the page as situations that possibly only he in all of history accumulated. But what I want to focus on is the next chapter. Paul uses such agonizing language for this next experience of hardship.

Paul talks about himself in 2 Corinthians 12 as being one who has received wonderful visions from God. He is defending his apostleship for much of 2 Corinthians in order to defend the message God gave through him.

In verse 7 and following, he writes,

> So to keep me from becoming conceited because of the surpassing greatness of the revelations, a thorn was given me in the flesh, a messenger of Satan to harass me, to keep me from becoming conceited. Three times I

pleaded with the Lord about this, that it should leave me. But he said to me, "My grace is sufficient for you, for my power is made perfect in weakness." Therefore, I will boast all the more gladly of my weaknesses, so that the power of Christ may rest upon me. For the sake of Christ, then, I am content with weaknesses, insults, hardships, persecutions, and calamities. For when I am weak, then I am strong. (2 Corinthians 12:7-12)

No one knows what the thorn in the flesh is. Paul seems to intentionally not define it. It has been guessed at by many theologians over the years. Some think it's a physical sickness or ailment, particularly his eyesight deteriorating. When I read it, I feel like it has to be a form of Obsessive Compulsive Disorder. I imagine for those who know complicated grief, they read their story, too. Beautifully, we don't know what it is specifically and thus can identify with it broadly.

A few things to point out.

1. A thorn was given to accomplish the good of helping him not become proud. Pride is the great enemy of spiritual formation as it elevates the ego to a place where there is simply less room for God. The grace of suffering that Paul was given was to preserve a humility of soul that is the great friend to any who seek to truly live in communion with him.

2.The thorn was a source of harassment and caused Paul to plead with God to take it away multiple times. Paul has just mentioned a lot of terrible things that happened in his life in the previous chapter. He details them without much emotional language. Paul is not an exaggerator but is one of the more matter of fact personalities in the New Testament. his language here demonstrates the immense discomfort that he underwent without the rescue of God. If it has Paul pleading multiple times, it is not a small cross he is carrying.

3.Undoubtedly, this thorn was not an efficient thing in his life; it led to less time and energy to preach, write and accomplish ministry. Paul was an instrument that God used mightily, but his accomplishments in ministry were not more important than his purity of soul. God did not fix the problem to get Paul back on the campaign. He took the time of suffering to work out the things of his soul. Oh, what balm this passage has been to me as I have wondered why God would allow such internal pain to me as a pastor. It makes me walk slower, like all limps do. It forces me to not work tireless hours. It beats me to a point where what I have feels like not enough. Paul demonstrates that God would rather have broken and responsive leaders than gifted or highly productive ones. This has been lived out in so many suffering pastors and leaders across our world.

4.The good of the thorn was that it forced Paul to experience his own weakness and, because of that, the power of God. Paul directly quotes God himself.

But he said to me, "My grace is sufficient for you, for my power is made perfect in weakness." (2 Corinthians 12:9)

God credits the perfecting work of his own power to be lived out in the human. How? He does this by going to the place of their greatest need and weakness. It is on this stage that his power is most fully and perfectly displayed and experienced.

5.While all of the above is true, this assigned torment was a messenger of Satan and shared the qualities of great agony and cruelty that any messenger of hell would carry. Was this a good thorn? Was it something that had inherent glory itself? No. It was the dark messenger of Satan that distorted the good design of God that the human would live in fullness of joy. This temporary messenger of hell was not "good", but it was used by God to construct a deeper and more meaningful trust in him. Such is the way of Christian suffering. The glory of God is that he uses awful things like crosses to construct the structural foundation of the Kingdom of Heaven.

****

The list of those who knew external and internal suffering in the Bible is both brutal and beautiful. We focused in on three briefly, but we could look much deeper into the stories of Job, Jesus, Peter, Hannah, Mary, the bleeding woman in Luke 8, Samuel, Simeon, the unhealed blind man in John 6 and countless others. Each of their stories speaks to levels of affliction that are severe and painful. Each of them speaks a testimony to the glory of God, who uses even suffering to draw his people near.

Prayer for the Sojourners of Biblical Sufferers

Suffering Son,
I want to live healthy and whole, unpunctured by the thorns of hell.
Give me grace to partner with you as these people did.
But not just with you. Also, with them. They bear a witness that I am able to join.

Faithful Father,
Thank you for the humanity of the Scriptures. It reads so guttural and includes such messes that it becomes clearer and clearer over time, that real life, real pain, real affliction is part of the real story.

Near Spirit,
Who has loved and led so many suffering servants, let my voice join the choir of the afflicted witness that says
"You are God who sees and hears"
"You are God of the light and God of the dark"
"You are God that writes his story with blood and thorn"
"You are even here, at the far side of the sea"

4

FELLOWSHIP OF THE TORMENTED IN CHRISTIAN HISTORY

Anxiety, grief, depression, insecurity and severe bouts of internal pain are not new experiences for the followers of Jesus. While pilgrims of Christ have known for centuries of the great joys, revelations, miracles and answered prayer requests, they also have known the confusion and agony of the dark. I am highlighting four people whose names you have most likely heard. They are among the names of people that I refer others to when they feel like what they're experiencing is too painful to be considered a part of the Christian life. Each of these people have had many books written about them in much greater detail than what I can do here. I include the following people for three reasons. 1) Because they give language to the struggle.   2) Because they are people that most of us already know and trust. We have learned the character of God through their stories, books, lifestyles and teaching. We also benefit from how they have responded to the internal struggle in their lives. 3) Because they each struggle with mental and emotional pain, but they do so in different ways. I have intentionally not provided some sort of list of all that hurts the inside of a person. To do so would be to inevitably ignore some of the very personal ailments of the mind and heart. However, while each of these dear people shared in great mental and emotional loss, they did so in their own unique way. I pray that you can, like me, find solace in their stories and hope from their Christ.

Lastly, I want to reiterate that I do not know of an official diagnosis for any of these friends, and I want to remind us that interior pain is not only caused by chemical imbalances or disorders. Mental and emotional suffering can be caused by mental illness but that is neither the cause of all interior pain nor is it the only way to address the situation. One does not need a neurological abnormality to experience the agonies of discouragement, grief, loneliness and relational rejection.

God used Charles Spurgeon to speak to me personally in a period of questioning whether I could stay in the ministry. My counseling pastor took me to him and graciously said to me, "Ben, it has been my experience that this is the normal way that God prepares ministers. It is through suffering."

The Depression of Charles Spurgeon:

Charles Spurgeon (1834-1892) is known as the "Prince of Preachers." He preached to over 10,000,000 people in his lifetime (without YouTube) and has written books that have stood the test of time and remain in print today.[20]

I once was in a bookstore that had a bust of Charles Spurgeon and it struck me how ridiculous that he would think it was. It also struck me that he had a giant head. God stuffed that ample sized skull with a wonderful mind and gift for language. While he had basically no formal training, he often preached 12 times per week and mentored hundreds of other pastors while serving his own congregation.

Charles Spurgeon spoke and wrote about his depression with jarring honesty. He is an advocate for those who experience darkness like this and was willing to use his own story to help others find some relief. It is no small fete for a man to preach to millions of people who did not suffer like he did. The simplest way for any preacher to speak is to try to connect with the felt needs of the people they are preaching to and to hide their own felt needs if they differ. Spurgeon spoke with such candor from his own story, regardless if it was shared by others or not. It has given preachers who struggle with depression all over the world a place of safety and understanding. By his declaration of 1) the sufficiency of Christ and 2) the devastation of depression, he has loosed the tongues of many of us to be able to give testimony of the coexistence of both of those things.

Spurgeon did not mince words at how difficult depression was for him.

> I have suffered many times from severe sickness and frightful mental depression seeking almost to despair. Almost every year I've been laid aside for a season, for flesh and blood cannot bear the strain, at least such flesh and blood as mine.[21]

And in another instance,

> I am the subject of depressions of spirit so fearful that I hope none of you ever get to such extremes of wretchedness as I go to.[22]

Spurgeon knew great physical pain. He had a host of medical conditions that were a plague to him. These included gout, rheumatism, smallpox and Bright's disease.[23] His most lengthy and difficult physical suffering was from gout, from which he suffered from age 35 until the end of his life.[24] He used that physical pain to further identify with those struggling with the pain of the mind.

> We very speedily care for bodily diseases; they are too painful to let us slumber in silence, and they soon urge us to seek a physician or a surgeon for our healing. Oh, if we were as much alive to the more serious wounds of our inner man.[25]

And in another instance,

> Personally, I know that there is nothing on earth that the human frame can suffer to be compared with despondency and prostration of mind.[26]

Spurgeon's story reminds us that depression is not a sin. It is not simply the unwillingness of the person to choose happiness instead of sorrow. Depression is not necessarily the fruit of a lack of trust or a backsliding faith. Depression is a cross that many in this life have to carry. Spurgeon teaches us that suffering of this type is not outside way to the Christian growth; it was the school that Christ used to train him to be a pastor.

> I am afraid that all the grace I have got from my comfortable and easy times and happy hours might almost lie on a penny. But the good I have received from my sorrows, pains, and griefs is altogether incalculable. Affliction is . . . the best book in a minister's library.[27]

And in another instance,

> I venture to say that the greatest earthly blessing that God can give to any of us is health, with the exception of sickness. Sickness has frequently been of more use to the saints of God than health has. . .. A sick wife, a newly-made grave, poverty, slander, sinking of spirit might teach lessons nowhere else to be learned so well. Trials drive us to the realities of religion.[28]

Spurgeon, ever the teacher, offers insight on how to deal with people who are in the throes of depression. He looks out for them and warns us against misunderstanding the pain of those near us. By doing so, he has cared for the many who suffer in this way. I had not seen this quote until recently when reading Zach Eswine's book, *Spurgeons Sorrows; Realistic Hope for Those Who Suffer from Depression*[29]. These words would have been such a friend to me and an aid to those near me when I was in the darkest of my depression. May it be a reminder to each of us as we go through very painful seasons.

> Especially judge not the sons and daughters of sorrow. Also, no ungenerous suspicions of the afflicted, the poor, and the despondent. Do not hastily say they ought to be more brave, and exhibit a greater faith. Ask not - 'why are they so nervous, and so absurdly fearful?' No ... I beseech you, remember, you understand not your fellow man.[30]

I can't wait to talk with Spurgeon in heaven. I long to hear how the great orator would articulate what it was like to gain the gifts of eternal undimmed communion. I long even more to hear of the joy that was his when he was freed from the bonds of internal pain that he knew on earth. There, I want to thank him for having the back of so many of us with the words that he left behind.

> Knowing by most painful experience what deep depression of spirit means, being visited therewith at seasons by no means few or far between, I thought it might be consolatory to some of my brethren if I gave my thoughts thereon, that younger men might not fancy that some strange thing had happened to them when they became for a season possessed by melancholy; and that sadder men might know that one upon whom the sun has shone right joyously did not always walk in the light.[31]

The Grief and Loneliness of C.S. Lewis:

While I was growing up, I had a hard time imagining C.S. Lewis as a real person. He is perhaps the most influential Christian mind of the last 100 years, and he always seemed larger than life to me. If one wanted to prove a point in my church, you needed a parable from Jesus and a quote from C.S. Lewis. There was no way that guy ate a normal breakfast or ever sat in traffic.

He is one of the most well-known Christian apologists in history and he brilliantly brought reason back into the discussion of faith. His writings have always been influential to me, and I didn't care if he was just a brain in a glass jar in England. His books were life changing.

It turns out he also was a real person. He spoke honestly of his own aversion to interior pain.

In one is his famous works called *The Problem of Pain*, Lewis, who was forty at the time of writing, tackles the question of every sufferer, if there is a loving God, why would he include so much pain in our stories? It is deep, philosophical, theological and brilliant. There is also a single page tucked in a later chapter that speaks to his own experience. It's my favorite page of the book. It is a description of how he himself dealt with internal pain.

> You would like to know how I behave when I am experiencing pain, not writing books about it. You need not guess, for I will tell you; I am a great coward. But what is that to the purpose? When I think of pain—of anxiety that gnaws like fire and loneliness that spreads

out like a desert, and the heartbreaking routine of monotonous misery, or again of dull aches that blacken our whole landscape or sudden nauseating pains that knock a man's heart out at one blow, of pains that seem already intolerable and then are suddenly increased, of infuriating scorpion-stinging pains that startle into maniacal movement a man who seemed half dead with his previous tortures—it 'quite o'ercrows my spirit'. If I knew any way of escape, I would crawl through sewers to find it. But what is the good of telling you about my feelings? You know them already: they are the same as yours. I am not arguing that pain is not painful. Pain hurts. That is what the word means. I am only trying to show that the old Christian doctrine of being made 'perfect through suffering' is not incredible. To prove it palatable is beyond my design.[32]

There is not a word wasted on that page and I wish he had written more. He writes that pain renders him a coward willing to do anything to escape it.

I had come to love the God Lewis describes in his other works with all my heart. But the humanity of the man on this page I understood in my very bones.

It is notable how he ends this discourse. He said, "To prove it palatable is beyond my design." The "it" he is referring to is Christian suffering. The suffering he is most describing above is his mental and emotional pain of anxiety and loneliness. If C.S. Lewis, the godfather of all sermon quotes and Christian explanations, is unable to make pain palatable … it shows us how deeply painful it truly is. It also is a relief that we don't have to always find words to describe the depths of the experience. If Lewis wasn't able to provide a way out through language, we can rest assured we will not either.

In this work, *The Problem of Pain*, he also writes of the awareness of God we are gifted from suffering.

> Pain insists upon being attended to. God whispers to us in our pleasures, speaks in our conscience, but shouts in our pain: it is His megaphone to rouse a deaf world.[33]

C.S. Lewis wrote another book about internal pain. This book was specifically about his own journey with grief. It was much later in his life after tragically losing his wife to illness. He wrote *A Grief Observed* under a pseudonym but it is widely known that it was he who wrote it. It is a deeply personal work of Lewis chronicling his experience. He wrote,

> No one ever told me that grief felt so like fear. I am not afraid, but the sensation is like being afraid. The same fluttering in the stomach, the same restlessness, the yawning. I keep on swallowing.
>
> At other times, it feels like being mildly drunk or concussed. There is a sort of invisible blanket between the world and me. I find it hard to take in what anyone says. Or perhaps, hard to want to take it in. It is so uninteresting. Yet I want the others to be about me. I dread the moments when the house is empty. If only they would talk to one another and not to me." [34]

He has deep insight into another dynamic of internal pain. He talks about the echo chamber that suffering makes in the mind.

He writes,

> Part of every misery is, so to speak, the misery's shadow
> or reflection: the fact that you don't merely suffer but
> have to keep on thinking about the fact that you suffer. I
> not only live each endless day in grief, but live each day
> thinking about living each day in grief.[35]

It seems that C.S. Lewis lived in the dark for seasons of his
life. Spurgeon seemed to live there perhaps more often than
Lewis did, but the dark is painful and disorienting no matter if it
is a visit for a long season or a more permanent stay. We are
indebted to both of their language describing their experience
regardless of how long they had been in that space.

Similar to Spurgeon, Lewis began to see great growth in his
life because of the pain that he went through. He came to know
the value that was only to be found in this grief. He writes of the
power of grief to understand his own frailty.

> God has not been trying an experiment on my faith or
> love in order to find out their quality. He knew it already.
> It was I who didn't. In this trial, He makes us occupy the
> dock, the witness box, and the bench all at once. He
> always knew that my temple was a house of cards. His
> only way of making me realize the fact was to knock it
> down.[36]

The Spiritual Darkness of Mother Teresa

Spurgeon said that the most hopeless darkness was spiritual
darkness. This type of darkness has been described by mature
saints for centuries. It has been called the "Cloud of

Unknowing" or the "Dark Night of the Soul." David himself provided a vivid language of thirsty, deserted land to describe this long season of spiritual life when one is not able to find God. If you have not had that experience, it is not complicated to describe but it is hard to understand. This is an experience where God seems absent, uninvolved and offers no clue of what he is up to. He frustrates more than He comforts. It is devastating and feels like destruction and abandonment. Mother Teresa went through this experience for years of her ministry. She prayed. She cried out to God to make his presence known and for long seasons of her life, He did not. He would not.

Mother Teresa won the Nobel Peace Prize in 1979 after decades of service. Originally from Albania, she felt a call on her life from Christ at age 12. She entered the monastery in Calcutta, India. After serving there for many years and having sweet communion with God, she requested to leave to go to the poorest slums of Calcutta. She went without any help or financial support. Over the decades that followed, she served thousands of people and many came to join her work. She became internationally known as her missionary society reached around the world serving the poor. She died in 1997 at the age of 87. Her face was worn with the toil of working in difficult conditions and by deep smile lines.

Most of the knowledge of this darkness she experienced was held back from people who followed and loved her. After her death, many of her personal correspondences were published in a book titled, *Come Be My Light*. Her writings were so significant that they mobilized both her supporters and detractors. Her supporters found these to be honest statements of faith in the midst of great service to God and the poor. Her detractors said that these seismic quotes revealed that she was not close to him in the first place. Count me among the supporters. Spiritual darkness is a frequently used method of God of dissembling and reassembling our faith, and it is most normative for those with great amounts of it.

Time Magazine noticed in her detailed later personal communications that the absence of God was felt most deeply.

> That absence seems to have started at almost precisely the time she began tending the poor and dying Calcutta and–except for a five-week break in 1959–never abated. Although perpetually cheery in public, the Teresa of the letters lived in a state of deep and abiding spiritual pain. In more than 40 communications, many of which have never before been published, she bemoans the "dryness," "darkness," "loneliness," and "torture" she is undergoing.[37]

Mother Teresa writes in one communication to Archbishop Perier,

> There is so much deep contradiction in my soul. Such deep longing for God - so deep that it is painful - a suffering continual - and yet not wanted by God - repulsed - empty - no faith - no love - no zeal. Souls hold no attraction - Heaven means nothing - to me, it looks like an empty place - the thought of it means nothing to me and yet this torturing longing for God. Pray for me, please, that I keep smiling at Him in spite

of everything. For I am only His - so He has every right over me. I am perfectly happy to be nobody, even to God. . . .Your Devoted Child in J.C. [Jesus Christ]

She wrote to Father Joseph Neuner, S.J., in an undated letter presumed to be written in April of 1961,

The place of God in my soul is blank—There is no God in me.

In the darkness...Lord, my God, who am I that You should forsake me? …

The one You have thrown away as unwanted—unloved.

I call, I cling,

I want—and there is no One to answer—no One on Whom I can cling; no, No One. Alone. The darkness is so dark—and I am alone.[38]

These words are hard to read. The length of her dark night is as long and as deep as anyone that I have read. Yet, even in the midst of this, she spoke to others of God's nearness and love for them.

Jesus wants me to tell you again...how much is the love He has for each one of you-beyond all what you can imagine...Not only He loves you, even more--He longs for you. He misses you when you don't come close. He thirsts for you. He loves you always, even when you don't feel worthy...[39]

She maintained profound trust and love for God in the midst of hearing so little in return. She wrote this incredible statement of identification with Christ after years of silence.

For the first time in these 11 years--I have come to love

the darkness--for I believe now that it is a part, a very, very small part of Jesus' darkness and pain on earth. You have taught me to accept it [as] a 'spiritual side of 'your work.'[40]

Mother Teresa is an overwhelming example of obedience to Christ even when he offers so little felt consolation. Her commitment that he was real and that she did know him deeply could survive decades of personal desert. Her words echo the Psalms, ever concluding her commitment to trust and accept God even when she could not understand where He was or what He was doing. That level of trust is other-worldly. I know of very few examples in the history of the church that mirror it.

The Insecurity and Identity Struggle of Henri Nouwen

The above three people have meant a great deal to me in my life as mentors and teachers. Henri Nouwen is more than that to me. He has become a friend to my soul. His words of the inner life have been a guide and a comfort to me more than any other. If he and I were to talk about theology, we would not agree on everything. Still, I don't think either of us would care, because we would be too busy simply talking about what our Jesus is like in the throes of our inner struggle, how he loves and how he works, how he frustrates us and how he ultimately brings us back to his heart of love in his time. The One that Nouwen talks about is the One my soul loves.

Henri Nouwen was a brilliant man. He was a professor at Oxford University and Notre Dame. He authored many books. In each of his works, he writes about the love of God meeting us in our place of human need. He deeply felt that the minister must be an "articulator of inner events".[41] He has been that articulator for many.

> The key word here is "articulation." Those who can articulate the movements of their inner lives, who can give names to their varied experiences, need no longer be victims of themselves... They are able to create space for the Spirit, whose heart is greater than their own, whose eyes see more than their own, and whose hands can heal more than their own.[42]

Nouwen was honest about his difficulty connecting with his father, a wound that he carried with him. He wrote often of the insecure disposition that he had and the deep feelings of loneliness that he knew. He talked about these as wounds. It was through these wounds that he sought and experienced the love of God that transformed his life.

Henri Nouwen went through deep anguish after experiencing abandonment from a close friend. He kept a daily journal during that time. For 8 years, he was not ready to publish the journal entries as he feared them to be too raw and personal. Eventually, these writings were published and called *The Inner Voice of Love*. He wrote these journal entries to himself as he fiercely clung to God's love in his own insecurity and pain.

> Every time you do something that comes from your needs for acceptance, affirmation, or affection, and every time you do something that makes these needs grow, you know that you are not with God. These needs will never be satisfied; they will only increase when you yield to

them.

> Not being welcome is your greatest fear. It connects with your birth fear, your fear of not being welcome in this life, and your death fear, your fear of not being welcome in the life after this. It is the deep-seated fear that it would have been better if you had not lived.[43]

Nouwen also reminds us that no level of success or accolade can insulate us from soul-deep questions of personal identity.

> You will hear voices saying, "You are worthless, you have nothing to offer, you are unattractive, undesirable, unlovable." The more you sense God's call, the more you will discover in your own soul the cosmic battle between God and Satan. Do not be afraid. Keep deepening your conviction that God's love for you is enough, that you are in safe hands, and that you are being guided every step of the way. Don't be surprised by the demonic attacks. They will increase, but as you face them without fear, you will discover that they are powerless.[44]

Nouwen is a profound example of a person who is willing to lovingly host the youngest and most painful parts of himself. For so many of us, these are parts we are ashamed of, protect at all costs and desperately try to hide from even ourselves. In this way, Nouwen was a man of profound courage and compassion. He wrote to himself,

> Your pain is deep, and it won't just go away. It is also uniquely yours because it is linked to some of your earliest

life experiences. Your call is to bring that pain home. As long as your wounded part remains foreign to your adult self, your pain will injure you as well as others. Yes, you have to incorporate your pain into yourself and let it bear fruit in your heart and the hearts of others.[45]

Nouwen was known to frequently reach out to others. He was a profound example of sharing with others his pain. His difficulty was not in hiding; however, he struggled to not have other people solve his pain. He spoke of the profound need to not let others do the work for him.

The main question is, "Do you own your pain?" As long as you do not own your pain—that is, integrate your pain into your way of being in the world—the danger exists that you will use the other to seek healing for yourself. When you speak to others about your pain without fully owning it, you expect something from them that they cannot give. As a result, you will feel frustrated, and those you wanted to help will feel confused, disappointed, or even further burdened.[46]

Like Spurgeon, Nouwen uses the language of the cross to describe our work with Christ.

This is what Jesus means when he asks you to take up your cross. He encourages you to recognize and embrace your unique suffering and to trust that your way to salvation lies therein. Taking up your cross means, first of all, befriending your wounds and letting them reveal to you your own truth.[47]

***

I want to share my experience of writing this chapter and sitting with these dear people of God. When I started reading in preparation for writing this chapter, I found myself comforted in the words and shared experiences of these saints. The words of Lewis and Nouwen, particularly, have long been like two strong splints on a broken leg for me. They have provided support and protection for me over the course of my internal struggle. They have helped me safely gain strength when I could not take steps without help. Their words have nurtured and healed me.

Yet, as I continued reading and writing with these four dear souls, I had a tremendous sadness come over me. It was much darker than I was anticipating and lingered longer than I wanted. It hit me on three layers. The first one was personal.

I found myself fearing that I will suffer as long as Spurgeon. His words are so beautiful but so painful. I have lived in that level of depression but only in one season of my life. I never want to experience that level of pain again. I found myself wondering if heaven would close up for me like it did for Mother Theresa. I can't imagine learning to love the dark after 11 years of hearing so little from God. That terrifies me. I fear the pains, anxieties and griefs of this life will be with me as long as they were with these spiritual guides I have come to love. I felt like a lost child in a large store as I sat with these sufferers. It was a feeling of helplessness and acute awareness that I don't know how to avoid something bad from happening. I hate mental and emotional pain and reading of theirs made me fear for more of my own.

In the second layer of processing, I found myself grieving and wanting to cry "unfair" for how much pain they had in this world. Being legends like C.S. Lewis or Charles Spurgeon did not mean they were not people. It feels so wrong that someone like Nouwen, who has given such wisdom and freedom to people in pain, was tethered to pain himself. When Mother Teresa was the very hands of God to people, how could God withhold his own loving hands from her? These teachers' wounds lasted years and sometimes decades. They wrote their lessons and stories in their own blood and with the tears of long sleepless nights. I am so grateful for their example and invaluable language to the struggle, but I wish they didn't have to go to hell to get it.

The last layer was you. I imagined a reader of this book. First I imagined people that I know that might read it: people who know pain in their insides that somehow feels hollow and overwhelmingly heavy at the same time. I don't want them to struggle with their affliction anymore. If I were God, I would have lifted them out by now. I don't have a strong enough stomach to watch them suffer this long.

Then I thought of who might read this that I don't know.

I imagined this book in the hands of the lonely, the afraid, the depressed, ones with aching bones and broken hearts. My heart was heavy remembering that there are so many people who live like that. This world has so much sorrow.

This all was like a chasm for me, and I was on the cusp of it, kicking rocks over the ledge. I felt grateful that I was not in utter despair, but I felt on the edge of it. Then I felt like I didn't want the flimsy foothold of hope anymore. Hope is life itself to those who are internally afflicted, but it also carries with it the great fear of being hurt again. These four saints are gone, along with many others who knew this level of pain. I know this all sounds very dark, but what we are talking about are not stories that are just buttoned up and in the past. It is the reality that many face on this very day. It may be your reality today. These four saints are gone, along with many others who knew this level of pain. But, they have been replaced by many others who are currently living with these agonies. I am so sorry if that is you.

The last thing I felt as I worked on this chapter was deep kinship. I have felt close to Spurgeon, Lewis, Mother Teresa and Nouwen. I have felt close to those who know the suffering that they knew. I have felt close to you, the fellowship of the tormented. You all are heroes of mine. We make up a hobbled army. At times, we feel like we are just like every other person. At other times, we feel like we are blessed to know our way with Christ, even in the dark. At other times we are begging that Christ would take this cross from us. We know lots of "times", but we keep going, with plenty of limping, second guessing, laughing at ourselves and crying when it is just too much.

I want to end this chapter with a view of heaven.

In that place, Spurgeon knows no more physical or mental torture. He no longer gazes into the abyss of the English Channel, clinging to his lasts bits of weathered hope. He now stares into the glory of Christ, eyes lit with joy and mirth. I imagine him still smoking his giant cigar there, too. I think of Lewis, who is no longer reduced to the feelings of a coward in the face of his grief and anxiety. He doesn't have to wrestle with pain theologically and philosophically for himself or us anymore. He is with his wife. Mother Theresa knows unbroken fellowship with the Christ she married on earth. There are no more lessons to be taught or learned by the teacher of silence. She is fully with him and He with her. Henri Nouwen feels loved and safe. Completely. He is freed from the wounds of insecurity and loneliness that fettered him on earth. He wrote about the word 'home' so often. I am so glad he has fully arrived.

I think about you and me, who are not there yet. Our questions are not resolved. Our uncertainties remain uncertain. Our timeline of the seasons of interior pain does not have an end date that we can see. We travel this world of faith and mental health on its precarious path and don't always know how much more we can take. Forgive me if I'm being dramatic, but sincerely, I cannot wait for Heaven with you. I can't wait to see what we shall gain there and what we shall leave behind. I long to speak to you there of how He got us through the very times that we thought were too deep, too wide, too long and too high for us to endure. I long to hear how he showed us then and for eternity that his love was deeper, longer, wider and higher still. Dear "weary traveler, you won't be weary long"[48].

<u>The Chorus of the Tormented</u>

One day You'll make everything new, Jesus
One day You will bind every wound
The former things shall all pass away
No more tears
One day You'll make sense of it all, Jesus
One day, every question resolved
Every anxious thought left behind
No more fear
One day, we will see face to face Jesus
Is there a greater vision of grace
And in a moment, we shall be changed
On that day
And one day we'll be free, free indeed, Jesus
One day, all this struggle will cease
And we will see Your glory revealed
On that day
And when we all get to heaven
What a day of rejoicing that will be
When we all see Jesus
We'll sing and shout the victory
We will weep no more
No more tears, no more shame
No more struggle, no more
Walking through the valley of the shadow
No cancer, no depression
Just the brightness of Your glory
Just the wonder of Your grace

Everything as it was meant to be
All of this will change
When we see You face to face
Jesus, face to face
When we all get to heaven
What a day of rejoicing that will be
When we all see Jesus
We'll sing and shout the victory[49]

20 Taylor, Justin. "Charles Spurgeon's Battle with Depression". The Gospel Coalition Blogs: Evangelical History. May 19th, 2022. https://www.thegospelcoalition.org/blogs/evangelical-history/charles-spurgeons-battle-with-depression/

21This was referenced in *Encouragement for the Depressed; Charles Spurgeon* (Wheaton, IL: Crossway, 2020). They cited this "From an address by Spurgeon on May 19, 1879. Cited in Ernest LeVos, C.H. Spurgeon and the Metropolitan Tabernacle (iUniverse, 2014).

22 Spurgeon, Charles, "Joy and Peace in Believing," *Metropolitan Tabernacle Pulpit (MTP),* Vol 12, Sermon 692 (http://www.spurgeonsgems.org/vols10-12/chs692.pdf), Accessed August 3rd, 2023.

23 Taylor, Justin. "Charles Spurgeon's Battle with Depression". The Gospel Coalition Blogs: Evangelical History. May 19th, 2022. https://www.thegospelcoalition.org/blogs/evangelical-history/charles-spurgeons-battle-with-depression/

24 Dr Amundsen, Darrel. "The Anguish and Agonies of Charles Spurgeon". Christian History Issue #29, 1991. Accessed https://christianhistoryinstitute.org/magazine/article/anguish-and-agonies-of-charles-spurgeon)

25 Spurgeon, Charles Haddon. *Healing for the Wounded.* New Park Street Pulpit Volume 1. Accessed https://www.spurgeon.org/resource-library/sermons/healing-for-the-wounded/

26Eswine, Zach. *Spurgeon's Sorrows. Realistic Hope for Those Who Suffer from Depression.* (Scotland, UK: Christian Focus Publications Ltd. 2014).

27Alcorn, Randy. *We Shall See God; Charles Spurgeon's Classic Devotional Thoughts on Heaven.* (Carol Stream, IL: Tyndale House Publishers Inc., 2011).

28 Spurgeon, Charles. *An All-Round Ministry; Addresses to Ministers and Students.* (Waterford, Ireland: Passmore and Alabaster, 1886.)

29 Eswine, Zach. *Spurgeon's Sorrows. Realistic Hope for Those who Suffer from Depression.* (Scotland, UK: Christian Focus Publications Ltd. 2014).

30Spurgeon, Charles. *Man Unknown to Man.* Metropolitan Tabernacle Pulpit Volume 24, April 13, 1889. Accessed https://www.spurgeon.org/resource-library/sermons/man-unknown-to-man/#flipbook/

31 Alcorn, Randy. "Depression, Gratitude and Charles Haddon Spurgeon. September 4th, 2007. https://www.epm.org/blog/2007/Sep/4/depression-gratitude-and-charles-haddon-spurgeon

[32] Lewis, C.S. *The Problem of Pain*. (San Francisco: Harper One, 2015)

[33] *Ibid.*

[34] Lewis, C.S. *A Grief Observed*. (New York, NY: Harper Collins, 2015)

[35] *Ibid.*

[36]*Ibid.*

[37] Biema, David Van. "Mother Teresa's Crisis of Faith." Tim Magazine, World. https://time.com/4126238/mother-teresas-crisis-of-faith/

[38] *Ibid.*

[39] *Mother Teresa; Come Be My Light; The Private Writings of the Saint of Calcutta.* Edited and with Commentary by Kolodiejchuk, Brian M.C. (New York, NY: Double Day, 2007)

[40]*Ibid.*

[41] Nouwen, Henri. The Wounded Healer: Ministry in Contemporary Society. New York, NY: Doubleday, 1972.

[42] *Ibid.*

[43] Nouwen, Henri J. M... The Inner Voice of Love: A Journey Through Anguish to Freedom. (New York, NY: Image Books Doubleday, 1996.

[44] *Ibid.*

[45] *Ibid.*

[46] *Ibid.*

[47] Nouwen, Henri. *Bread for the Journey: A Day book for Wisdom and Faith. San Francisco, CA*: Harper One, 2006).

[48] This is a beloved lyric taken from the song *Weary Traveler* by Jordan St. Cyr., 2021. CCLI #: 7184142

[49] Redman, Matt. [Song] *One Day (When We All Get to Heaven)*. CCLI 7091537.

5

THE GREATEST TREASURE OF CHRISTIAN SUFFERING

My wife is a therapist and works in a private practice near our home. She sees first hand what mental and emotional suffering does in peoples' lives. She watches the wake of destruction. She witnesses the miracle of new life coming up out of scorched earth.

She wisely recommended that I distinguish the suffering I am speaking about. Suffering can be a destructive or healing force in anyone's life, Christian or non, male or female, American or Iranian, young or old. That remains true in all walks of life in all of human experience. Suffering and the human response to it will define much of each of our lives.

What I am speaking about specifically is the work of suffering in the life of the Christian ('Christ one').

The unique thing about Christian suffering is not the suffering. It's the Christ.

Christian suffering offers the same gift that all Christian life is meant to offer - an opportunity to know God through *union with Christ*. It is another tool that does the same purpose. We have been made, sculpted, and designed for relationships. Union with God and his people is the primary gift that comes from the Christian life.

We started with John 17 in chapter one. Let's return. Here, Jesus prays to the Father and, in one chapter, he gives the "why" of the Gospel. This is the purpose for which he has come. He goes over, with the Father, the point of this whole mission one last time before he receives the cross the next day.

Jesus prays,

> I have revealed you to those whom you gave me out of the world. They were yours; you gave them to me and they have obeyed your word. Now they know that everything you have given me comes from you. For I gave them the words you gave me and they accepted them. They knew with certainty that I came from you, and they believed that you sent me. I pray for them. I am not praying for the world but for those you have given me, for they are yours. All I have is yours, and all you have is mine. And glory has come to me through them. I will remain in the world no longer, but they are still in the world, and I am coming to you. Holy Father, protect them by the power of your name, the name you gave me,

so that they may be one as we are one. While I was with them, I protected them and kept them safe by that name you gave me. None has been lost except the one doomed to destruction so that Scripture would be fulfilled.

I am coming to you now, but I say these things while I am still in the world, so that they may have the full measure of my joy within them. I have given them your word and the world has hated them, for they are not of the world any more than I am of the world. My prayer is not that you take them out of the world but that you protect them from the evil one. They are not of the world, even as I am not of it. Sanctify them by the truth; your word is truth. As you sent me into the world, I have sent them into the world. For them, I sanctify myself, that they too may be truly sanctified.

My prayer is not for them alone. I pray also for those who will believe in me through their message, that all of them may be one, Father, just as you are in me and I am in you. May they also be in us so that the world may believe that you have sent me. I have given them the glory that you gave me, that they may be one as we are one— I in them and you in me—so that they may be brought to complete unity. Then the world will know that you sent me and have loved them even as you have loved me.

Father, I want those you have given me to be with me where I am, and to see my glory, the glory you have given me because you loved me before the creation of the world.

Righteous Father, though the world does not know you, I know you, and they know that you have sent me. I have made you known to them, and will continue to make you known in order that the love you have for me may be in them and that I myself may be in them. (John 17:6-26)

Let's be honest, that's a long prayer. If your pastor tried to pull one off that was that long, you can only hope it was during a "you may be seated" moment. Some may have skipped ahead because of the length of the text. I challenge you to genuinely read it. Experience it.

As many times as I have discussed and enjoyed this prayer, I do not know a way to shorten it. The prayer folds over on itself, like a Neapolitan kneading pizza dough. "I in you," and "you in me," and "you in them," and "them in us," and "they with each other" cover the landscape of this prayer of Jesus. The word 'one' and the concept of 'oneness' is more in this text than at a New Age convention.

John, who records this prayer, is constantly mentioning how affectionately connected the Father, Son and Spirit are. John records in his gospel how Jesus communicates to his followers about the Father and the Holy Spirit. He is continuously speaking of their oneness. There is no union as intimate as the union of the Godhead. It is the ultimate example of "I in you," and "you in me," and "we with one another".

That is what Jesus is praying for—that the type of union that is known to the Father and Son would be the same type of union that would exist between Father, Son and us. That does not make us a fourth person of the Trinity, but it does graft us into the very dance of the Trinity. This ever folding into itself union with God in Christ is the whole point.

Relationship with God is worth all other things. Paul writes,

> But whatever were gains to me, I now consider loss for the sake of Christ. What is more, I consider everything a loss because of the surpassing worth of knowing Christ Jesus my Lord, for whose sake I have lost all things. I consider them garbage, that I may gain Christ... (Philippians 3:7-10)

This is not the stuff of master philosophers that Jesus and Paul are talking about. It is a relationship of deep knowing and true loving one another. It is a union of the self with God himself. It is connected, intimate and familiar.

It is what Christianity is. It is the story of how a group of persons went from separation to union with God.

J.I. Packer writes,

> Communion between God and man is the end to which both creation and redemption are the means; it is the goal to which both theology and preaching must ever point; it is the essence of true religion; it is, indeed, the definition of Christianity.[50]

In his book *Union with Christ; How to Know and Understand and Enjoy God*, Rankin Wilbourne writes,

> The greatest treasure of the gospel, greater than any other benefit of the gospel, is the gift of God himself. [51]

In this way, Christian suffering is no different from every other Christian experience. Christian suffering is another tool, another season in which to know Christ more. This is the same for seasons of blessing. All things in the Christian life serve this goal - that we may know and relate to him more. Mental and emotional suffering hurt like hellfire, but they serve the everlasting purpose for which we have been designed.

How does suffering unite us with Christ more? How can we know him even on the "far side of the sea" (Psalm 139:9). How can we, as we stumble around in mental and emotional distress, connect our fiery insides to a God who is all love?

The release of other attachments

The contemplatives give us profound insight into what it means to deeply know God. They often speak in terms of attachments. Attachments are secondary things that we use to try to find our primary sense of purpose and joy.

You and I have and will continue to attach ourselves to things of this world. Attachments are not primarily bad or superficial. Most of them are really good. But, these attachments turn to idols when we look to them as primary source of our identity and sense of happiness. They are things that need not always be deleted but reordered.

When good things such as my reputation, the financial security of my family, my desire to be known and loved by my peers, my desire for rest and comfort or even my holiness become the means by which I try to find my primary sense of self, I have made them into something that they were not made to be. I have misused good things to try to make them more than they are meant to be. And because of that they will always be less than what I have wanted.

Yet, I am continually drawn to attach to the things around me as my primary source of joy.

That used to bother me more than it does now. For a long time, I felt so much guilt about this propensity. It didn't stop it. I tried aggressively to release myself from earthly attachments, which often led me to find my sense of worth in my spiritual work ethic. I started to find my identity in how hard I was willing to fight my ego, forsake my reputation and give up on the pleasures of earth. When my OCD mixed with my "spiritual commitment", I became obsessive to rid myself of evil and fiercely choose the most noble things. It was not pretty; it was savagery to myself.

Guess what survived that tornado of half spiritual, half mental disordered thinking? My propensity to find my identity and comfort in my pet idols and attachments. If anything, I simply learned how to disguise them as much holier things than they are. I could not rid myself of these disordered affections.

I realize I might be much less successful than you are at reordering my loves. But, if I am honest with myself, I don't think I have ever gotten over myself on my own. Even when I have chosen some hard core spiritual disciplines, if they are of my own making, they remained only about me.

A spiritual matriarch in our church was warming up with the worship band one Sunday morning. They were singing a song that used the phrase, "Christ is enough for me". I know this woman. She bleeds this truth as much as anyone I know. Christ is enough for her.

Being a generation younger than she, I said to her, "Ruth, it seems to me you really believe this. I find that people in my generation - me included - sort of believe this. We believe 'Christ and ____ is enough for me'. Christ and my kids doing well is enough for me. Christ and having a stable job is enough for me. Christ and not undergoing loss is enough for me. Christ and I, being a respected Christian man/woman, is enough for me. But you are not like that. You actually believe that Christ is enough ...."

She literally waved her hand to stop me. I was trying to pay her a wonderful compliment, celebrating how she attained something which many of us a generation younger had not. She light-heartedly said, "Ben, we tried all those things, too. I have tried all the Christ and ____. It is only because they didn't work that I have come to believe that Christ alone is enough." Knowing some of her story and the freedom that she has found in her relationship with Christ through seasons of suffering and deep soul mining, this was a great relief to me. She didn't release her attachments to secondary things on her own, either.

I should also clarify that Ruth is not a type of ascetic who only wears camel hair, prays and chews on a crust of bread. She loves dancing, kayaking, watching her grandkids play soccer, leading Bible studies, and she could tell you the names of every player on the Villanova Wildcats basketball team. All of these things are delights to her, made more beautiful because they are in their proper place. Her attachment to Christ is the center and other things are most enjoyed when they are in their proper orbit.

C.S. Lewis wrote,

> Put first things first and second things are thrown in. Put second things first and you lose both first and second things.[52]

We will all look to our natural attachments until those attachments are proved unworthy and unhelpful to us. I am learning to not be surprised by my appetite for cheap joy or comfort nor my inability to will myself into wanting something better.

It is suffering that has most shown me the new and living way. It is through my own mental and emotional strife, when my attachments were shown to be so insufficient, that I ever learned to look for that which is eternal and truly life. It is as if my attachments to people, to ego, to the things I sought for happiness and peace were able to hold me when my life felt lighter. Yet, as the weight of this cross grew, they were not strong enough to hold the size of my need and struggle.

Suffering is this gift that shows us the weakness of our attachments. It is when the other things can no longer work to satisfy and Christ allows us to suffer their loss that our appetites change. The appetites don't decrease, they grow because we are being starved. The gift of this is that it can give us a voracious hunger for what is most real.

The increased appetite for our soul's truest attachment

My wife once said to me, "Psychology gives us such a gift. It gives us language and category to understand a lot of the dysfunction of the mind, emotions and relationships between people. But, the information does not fix a person. What fixes a broken person is only love. And there is no love like the love of God. People can never be counted on as the deepest source of love. There is a love that only God can constantly give."

Dallas Willard is a spiritual guide of mine. His teaching has become a profound witness of the goodness and treasure of God in Christ. Towards the end of Dallas Willard's life, he met and talked with many people. One of those people was Jim Wilder, who describes himself as a neuro-theologian. Jim worked with Jane Willard, Dallas's wife. She was both a therapist and spiritual director. Jim and Dallas grew close at the end of Dallas' life, and they talked about what it meant to live attached to God in a relationship of love.

> Dallas Willard sat across from me with tears in his eyes as he looked at the floor. Dallas had only weeks to live, but his tears were not for his own life. "What I have learned in the past year," he told me, "is more important than what I learned in the rest of my life. "But I have no time to write about it.... You need to write about this."[53]

Jim Wilder and Dallas continued to talk about how our attachment to Christ in its deepest emotional, spiritual, and neurological bond was the source of all Christian life. He writes,

> The only kind of love that helps the brain learn better character is attachment love. The brain functions that determine our character are most profoundly shaped by who we love...
>
> This realization brought Dallas to tears. If the quality of our human attachments creates human character, is it

possible that when God speaks of love, "attachment" is what God means?[54]

The love of God through our union with Christ Jesus has the power to drive out fear, overcome strongholds of sin, and repair the damage of our hurting souls. Our attachment and trust in God is the method of growth in the Christian life. If all we are doing is teaching our minds and shifting some habits, it is not the Christian life. The Christian life is union, attachment and nearness with God. All things flow from that connection.

Jesus said,

> Abide in me, and I in you. As the branch cannot bear fruit by itself, unless it abides in the vine, neither can you unless you abide in me. I am the vine; you are the branches. Whoever abides in me and I in him, he it is that bears much fruit, for apart from me you can do nothing.... As the Father has loved me, so have I loved you. Abide in my love. (John 15:4-5, 9)

This is the ultimate attachment that we have been designed for.

Attachment to God is Eternal Life

After Jesus gave one of his most intense teachings on his own supremacy, many people walked away. They literally said, "This is a hard saying; who can listen to it?" (John 6:60). As a result of this teaching, "many of his disciples turned back and no longer walked with him". (John 6:66).

Jesus turns around and sees the 12 men who stuck with him through a lot already.

So Jesus said to the twelve, "Do you want to go away as well?" Simon Peter simply answered him, "Lord, to whom shall we go? You have the words of eternal life and we have believed, and have come to know, that you are the Holy One of God." (John 6:67-68)

Peter straight up says, "Where can we go? We are willing to go there - or anywhere! We probably would go exactly there, but all we know is that eternal life is not there. It's here. We are not being holy guys, sticking with you because you need us or because we are all about virtue. We are here because you are the Christ and we cannot find eternal life anywhere else."

Jesus himself, in our passage in John 17, gave an explicit definition of eternal life. It's not a place we go to when we die. It's not the beautiful transaction of salvation. It is the purpose of those things and the rest of all Christian teaching. Eternal life is communion with God himself. Jesus says, "This is eternal life that they may know the one true God and Jesus Christ whom you have sent." (John 17:3)

Attachment to God is not what eternal life is about. It is the very definition of what eternal life is. Eternal life is communion with God himself.

Practice of Attachment: Entering at the place of suffering

If you have picked up this book and made it to this point, I am guessing that mental and emotional suffering are not alien to you. Perhaps they are more true of someone you love than your own experience, but love brings their experience into you.

This is a wonderful place to start practicing union - at the place

of the pain and frustration. Don't try to go to the spiritual parts
of your life, enter where you are hurting. Pray honestly and ugly
like David. Wrestle like Jacob with a God that seems to be
allowing things that are not fair. Enter with him where you are.
Believe in what God promised through Isaiah,

> I will give you the treasures of darkness
>
> and the hoards in secret places,
>
> that you may know that it is I, the Lord, the God of
> Israel, who calls you by your name. (Isaiah 45:3)

Also, we need to enter with him as we are. Are you a writer?
Write letters to God. Are you a nature buff? Walk or kayak and
pray. Are you a big texter? A person who is going through great
suffering that I met with recently told me that he texts Jesus all
day long. He set up a contact on his phone is continually texting
with him. Enter with him where you are, as you are, with what
you know. He will meet you there.

Practice of Attachment: Spiritual Direction

As we talk about union with God at the point of mental and
emotional struggle, we can still feel guarded and reluctant to go
to him. For someone who has had their trust hurt so many times,
it sounds difficult and scary to go to him with what feels most
vulnerable. Every relationship has to prove itself trustworthy, or
it's not going to have much staying power. That is true of our
trust of God, too.

I encourage you to find safe people who have learned God in
this way. I am a big advocate of spiritual direction. Spiritual
direction is the practice of making sense of this relationship

with God. It is helping to form trust and to go to places where Jesus may never have been in one's life. It is not seeking to conjure up God's presence of love in someone. It is the learning to see how God is actively working already. Spiritual direction also happens in coffee shops and living rooms all around the world without the title. If you have not known how to find Christ in the darkness before, seek safe people who have met God there. Hearing from someone else could be the first step in establishing some trust with God. As that attachment grows, you will know more and more how to turn to him in the dark.

Practice of attachment: in the mundane

This attachment with God is made for every day. It is meant for Tuesdays. It's meant for days when we are pleasantly surprised about our budget for the month and days when we suffer emotional or mental pain. It's meant for days when we are frustrated at work or disappointed with our waistline. It's meant for times when we get to have fun or rest from labor. It's meant to fit into errands in the car and getting ready for Friday night dinner.

I want to tell you of an experience with him that meant a lot to me. It was on such a normal day.

I went on a walk to pray. I was feeling unholy, disconnected and frustrated in my relationship with him that day. I went out to pray with the thought, "Well, since this is not going very well with us together right now, clearly, I am the problem". So, I went to ask God what I needed to fix. What sin needed confessing to bring us back to alignment? What life change was necessary so that the telescope of my heart could gain refocus on him instead of all this worrying about me. But more than any of that, I went out to hear a rebuke from God so that I could get it over with.

As I prayed and started to mine my life for what could be wrong, he spoke to me very clearly. It was not what I was expecting to hear from him. It rarely is. As clear as day, with words that were louder than audible, he said to me, "I love you". This shocked me that he would use this time of necessary surgery for simply an intimate moment. It was so real. He was so close.

I had this great sense of relief. I could undergo the knife with this one that my soul knows and loves. I could walk through what was coming next after such an assurance.

With deep gratitude and tears, I thanked him. I thanked him for his nearness and his gentleness. His soft touch was what my soul needed, even though it was the furthest thing from what I was looking for. I thanked him for his dealing kindly with this frustrated mess I came to him with.

And I told him that I was ready. With that deep reminder of his companionship, I could take the hard stuff. With that assurance of his presence, bring it on.

I asked him specifically to speak conviction into me so that I could repent and be brought back to deep sense of relationship. *Thank you for your love, now, what do I really need to hear?*

He spoke with undoubted clarity. "I love you". It was also clear that that was his only agenda today. It was the totality of what he wanted me to learn, to know, to digest or to process.

Here I was again convinced that this relationship with the divine was simply

a gospel of "sin management"[55]. Here he was, again, reminding me this is all about love.

Prayer for Union during emotional and mental suffering

Jesus, I am familiar with separation.
I know what it means to be separated from myself,
from others, from You.
More than that, I know what it feels like to be
disconnected in these ways.

Suffering entices me deeper into my aloneness. This is not
what I want, but it feels safer than risking
being together — even with you.
Show me a different way — a union-ed one.

Fold me in. In in You. You in me.
Father, Son, Spirit, I come to enter the dance
with all of my limp.
I am a nervous and do not know the steps and am not good at
shifting into your type of rhythm.
Grant me good humor and patience as I learned to practice
the clunky process of being united to you. Give me people who
are further in that I am to help show me the ways. Help me
remember that the first steps of learning and the last steps of
eternal mastery are a delight to both you and to me.

[50] Packer, J.I. *A Quest for Godliness: The Puritan Vision of the Christian Life.* (Wheaton, IL: Crossway Books, 1990)

[51] Wilburne, Rankin. *Union With Christ: The Way to Know and Enjoy God.* (Colorado Springs, CO: David C Cook, 2016.

[52] Lewis, CS. "First and Second Things". *God in the Dock: Essays on Theology and Ethics.* (Grand Rapids, MI: Eerdmans Publishing Company, 1994).

[53] Wilder, Jim. Renovated: God, Dallas Willard and the Church That Transforms. NavPress, Colorado Springs, 2020)

[54] *Ibid.*

[55] Willard, Dallas. *The Divine Conspiracy: Rediscovering Our Hidden Life in God.* New York, NY: Harper One, 1998).

6

THE SECONDARY TREASURES OF CHRISTIAN SUFFERING

The new Indiana Jones movie recently came out[56], proving once again that Harrison Ford will outlive us all. Indiana Jones is a franchise that started over 40 years ago about an archeologist professor who goes on wild adventures across the world. He has more lives than open shirt buttons. He is continually in peril as he rescues ancient artifacts from jungles and caves while navigating various ancient booby traps that are somehow mechanically sound 1000 years after they were constructed. Indiana survives these adventures with blood, sweat and tears ... and various relics that are of priceless value.

By the end of each movie, you are attached to his discovery because you realize what it took to find, discover and possess such a treasure. The process helps explain and validate the import of the thing that was found.

The mine of Christian suffering is as deep as it is dark, and the treasures found there are ones that become of great value to those who had to go there to find them. The goal of all Christian suffering is Christ himself but there are other priceless treasures found with him along the way. Their value to the sufferer cannot be overstated - not only because the process of discovering these was severe, but because returning to life the way it was before their discovery sounds as miserable as the suffering itself.

Below are five treasures that I have seen in my life as well as in the lives of other sojourners who have endured mental and emotional suffering. It should be noted that these treasures can be missed or avoided by those who go through this type of pain. Suffering never ensures growth. But these treasures are available in Christ if we are willing to partner with him in his work in us. They become visible if we are looking and the Guide brings us to them if we trust in his timing and process.

Treasure 1: Intimacy Forged at War

Emotional and mental suffering can isolate a person. This has many reasons.

1) It is exhausting and all of our energy goes to what feels like basic survival.

2) It gives the "Scarlet Letter of Neediness". Those who know the throes of this kind of suffering know that they come across as undone and unwell. They also know that it is not easy for

others to be their friend at times. No one wants to be a needy person. It is easier, at times, to be an unknown person.

3) It causes shame. It is so hard to look at oneself in the mirror during these seasons. It feels like you are being destroyed by an invisible force. In the beginning of difficult seasons, the internal soundtrack you may play is, "Maybe this thing I just thought of is the problem and if I fix it, all will be okay". This transitions over time to "There is no easy fix. It seems I am the problem". The level of shame and helplessness known there is very painful and isolating.

4) People who don't struggle this way cannot fully understand what it is like to go through this. This is not an indictment on them, but it is a reality. It is so demoralizing to be told simple solutions or trite suggestions for dealing with internal pain. After that risk has worked out poorly enough times, retreat is the natural mechanism that is triggered. And that mechanism is as mechanically sound as anything Indiana Jones ever faced.

Jesus, in his prayer in John 17, was not just focused on the blood-bought union of the person to God. He talked specifically of the blood-bought union that the family of God would have with each other. I have found these words very scary as I have dealt with all the reasons for isolation in my life. He prays,

> My prayer is not for them alone. I pray also for those who will believe in me through their message, that all of them may be one, Father, just as you are in me and I am in you. May they also be in us so that the world may believe that you have sent me. (John 17:20-21).

Jesus is talking about the oneness that He just used to describe the Godhead. He then speaks of that oneness as what happens in our union with him. But he is not done. His final prayer is that this oneness was to be experienced between one another.

Most of the New Testament is not written to individuals about how they should relate to God. Most of it is written to communities of faith on how they relate to each other and can know him together.

For the one who suffers with Christ, he will not let you only suffer alone with him. It's not how he designed it and he just won't lead you that way. Sufferers need flesh and bone. They need people to partner with them. Christ leads his people to his people.

Of course, someone who is mentally and emotionally struggling can opt to not do their work and depend on humans for things that humans cannot give. But, the temptation for many of us is to simply self protect because we don't risk the shame and fear of rejection.

I hate writing words that are anything but gentle to those in the throes of affliction. But I do feel a need to be direct as I say, do not let your fear keep you away from union with God's people. It is necessary to try and try again. You are not meant to carry this on your own. It is not the design or intent of your God that you do so.

The darkness of mental and emotional suffering gives you a chance to be vulnerable with your needs in a way that is terrifying, but if you see it through long enough, he will provide imperfect but safe people for you. Some of them will know similar pain. Many of them will not. Regardless, when love hits your aching vulnerability, there is a treasure to be found in people that is of incalculable value. There is an intimacy made at war that the Christian can deeply know and experience even while in pain.

This is always going to be a messy process.

For me, when I go through the worst of my struggle, I am asking myself, am I using this to separate from people who love me or connect me to them? I have a mantra that goes through my head, "when in doubt, reach out". In this process, I have overshared and undershared. I have been codependent and too independent. I have confused people who don't have pain like this and helped others understand what it is truly like to suffer in this way. I don't think the process of oneness is ever only smooth. It is never simple, easy or pain-free.

But it is worth it. Do not hide your pain from others. You have the chance in your pain to know closeness that you cannot without it. And it is through this - with the people of God - that we understand God himself better. It is an economy of oneness.

Eugene Petersen writes,

> Spiritual formation not only should not be - but also cannot be - professionalized. It takes place essentially in the company of friends and peers.[57]

I know there are those who read this who feel additional shame - "I don't do this well", "I am just a loner and now I hear that I am even doing my suffering wrong", or "My friends and peers feel more like they are skimming the surface and my experience with Christians feels more forced than it feels forged". If you hear nothing else, please hear this - keep looking. You may need a different church. You probably don't. You may need to have distance from some people for a time. You probably do. But, walk towards someone with this vulnerability, not away. Oneness is the stuff of love. True love can face the complex. It takes time, work, blood and a lot of grace. The result of such a life is the very stuff of the Godhead. That type of closeness can be known, if only in a fractured part, in a community with the family of God.

Treasure 2: Resilience Made One Revolution at a Time

My favorite picture of spiritual growth is a screw going into a piece of wood. The screw is the person. The wood is the love of God. As a screw goes into the wood, it goes in one turn/ revolution at a time. It is a slow and downward process - two words that I believe describe the normative experience of a person who is growing in their formation. As this happens, the screw goes through familiar cycles and patterns as it enters into the wood. This is true for us as we grow into Christ. We face similar things that we have before. We face similar seasons, are confronted with familiar insecurities, and are taken through old frustrations and pain. But, what growth is, what formation in Christ is, is that each time we pass through the same old season, we are driven a little deeper into the love of God. We are secured a little more. We find we are more and more ourselves as we are more and more anchored in his love.

Suffering is not all of life. But it is, for many of us who struggle with mental and emotional pain, a significant part of life. Sometimes, that season is shorter. Sometimes, it feels like forever. But, it is familiar. It can be scary when we hit triggers and stressful seasons that impact us and send us towards this struggle. When they come, we feel very young, reduced again to primal and defensive feelings.

But each time we enter, we also can remember that this is a season. We can remember that we have been here with Christ before. We have seen this barren landscape and he has not left before, nor will he this time either. Each time, it looks the same: emptied of hope and filled with potential terror. Each time, we are a bit more secure in knowing that God really is love and he will use this to pull us nearer and deeper. This, too, shall serve to unify us with him.

There are not many who feel brave and struggle like this. The felt experience is often weakness and fragility, like the feeling one gets after surgery when the anesthesia wears off. The threat is not welcomed or wanted. Relief is the only felt need.

Yet, through these seasons there is a tangible growth in resilience. Christ uses this to produce a power of courage and faith that is secured over time and struggle. These warriors have a security and strength that is so much greater than they themselves even recognize. Courage only counts when fear is present. These people know fear. They are also the fellowship of the most brave people I know.

Treasure 3: Freedom from the Illusion of Control

I was talking to a retired man in our church. He is one of those refreshingly honest people who probably could not withhold an opinion if he tried. He was telling me about someone he knew in his life. This person was younger but had a lot of things going for him, but not enough to impress my friend. He said about him, "You know, he is still young. He still believes that he has life by the [horns]". He didn't say horns. I instantly knew exactly what he was talking about. You know, those people who come across as entitled, proud and self-confident, believing that they can ensure a life through their own talent, effort and wisdom. For them, life is not a gift to be received. It is a privilege to be manipulated and formed in their image.

I can easily recognize that type of person because I am that type of person. Control issues run in my family and I have gladly taken the baton and run with it in ways that I have often been blind to.

Control breeds all kinds of ugly fruit of the false self:

1. Fear. Fear and control always operate together. Control is just the great effort we give to make sure that nothing we fear will ever happen to us. This could include being controlling in finances, image, or relationships. It could include controlling our spouse, children, employees, family, friends or people in the church. The controlling person is defensive because they are on high alert out of fear. The sad irony is that controlling people reproduce fear in their environments. They are not just driven by fear, they are manufacturers of it for those around them.

2. Comparison. Comparison always robs everyone of joy, but it does not mean that the controlling person won't use comparison to try and find it. For the controlling person, life is divided into winners and losers. The goal is winning,

and the way a controller finds out where they rank is by comparing against other people. Someone who is controlling is either despondent at each comparison or arrogant because of it. Either way is competitive, unsafe and far from love.

3. Resentment. The controlling person believes that "when something happens that it is out of my control, it simply should not have happened. It is unfair." Deep in the mind of controlling people is that they know how the world should operate and if you just would play along, this would work out okay. When things don't work out very well, then it's time to look for the person/God who messed up the perfect design the controller had in mind.

One of the hardest things about my own mental and emotional pain was that I could not fix it. This was a hard crash for me. I could not stop the wild thoughts. I could not rationally find someone that I knew I could blame. It just was. My mind did not cooperate, and my depression did not stop when I read my best Bible verses to it. I was not able to trust myself or my thinking. I had a helpless feeling that I could not get a firm grip on what was true or real, which painfully made me confront the fact that I am not a safe or sound master of my own fate. That is a terrifying feeling for someone who is trying to maintain control. I could not stop thoughts and feelings, much less shape my or anyone else's world. This pattern has been one that Christ has often used to bring me to my knees, fully out of control.

To say that this was or ever is a welcomed lesson to me is a lie. To lose a sense of control is scary and vulnerable. I hate it every time.

But when we are made to be in such a vulnerable place where we cannot fix ourselves, we are forced to recognize the folly of the illusion of control. C.S. Lewis writes about intended suffering and says,

> The creature's illusion of sufficiency must, for the creature's sake, be shattered.[58]

When we are free from this illusion, we learn to live each day as a gift, learning to live in the present rather than just setting up the future. For people who naturally live in the present, this may not sound like a significant shift, but for those who are constantly calculating outcomes and potential threats, it is truly a different way of existing in the world. It is a place of trust because choosing to be present is a way we accept our place and role in the world. Here we are not God, but are content in letting him have his own job. Here, we are not obsessed with potential outcomes that we can orchestrate. Here, the bonds of fear, comparison and resentment have less of a hold. Consequently, we also seem to pray a lot more.

Treasure 4: An Aversion to Depersonalized Religion

Depersonalized religion may sound like a subtle or inconsequential shift, but it has the potential to be very dangerous to the soul. Without suffering and the need to keep the first thing first, these tendencies happen to Christ's followers all of the time. We begin to make our faith about systems and organizational concerns more than personal and intimate ones. Our faith becomes about the things of faith. It becomes about

Christianity and not about Christ himself.

Our faith can become about the church. Our thoughts can become about how to grow the church, advance the church, or just complain about what is wrong with the church. We can begin to feel competitive with other churches, almost as if their losses could be our gain. Our faith can become more oriented to being an organization that we must perfect and protect at all costs. We may do this out of a desire to honor Christ, but even that is a little removed from living in active communion with him. In this, we act more like servants and less like his children. We also functionally begin to act as if Christ's mission in the world is all about our local faith community. When we talk, we talk more about what the church should be like than we talk about what Jesus himself is like.

Our faith can become about the country. We are in a dangerous time for that right now. Our mission in the world can become politically motivated. It is easy to get lost in a world of blogs and news sites. It is enticing in a competitive sense to keep fastidious track of when our side does something right, or their side makes a mistake. We tend to think that Jesus must be on this political side and anyone on the other side must not be with him. When we circle this drain long enough, we realize that we talk to our friends more about what our politicians are doing in our countries than about what Jesus is doing in us. If we continue on this path, We begin to look at our friends as allies or enemies based on their political affiliation. Christ is morphed into some earthly political movement not dissimilar to what most people wanted from him when he came in the early first century. This is happening in our day in an aggressive and combative way. Lord, have mercy.

Our faith can become about the Bible. Of course, our faith is built on what the Bible teaches. The Bible itself is of foundational value in the life of everyone who desires to know and follow the author of it. However, we can begin to focus on mastering the book and spend less time knowing its Hero. We can get lost in the minutia and get focused on small things in the text and engage in the very "stupid arguments" that we are warned against in the text (1 Timothy 2:23). These arguments are more about ego than they are about Scripture or about the one who wrote it. Tozer talks about the danger of this disposition in The Pursuit of God. He says,

> Self can live unrebuked at the very altar. It can watch the bleeding Victim die and not be in the least affected by what it sees. It can fight for the faith of the Reformers and preach eloquently the creed of salvation by grace, and gain strength by its efforts. To tell all the truth, it seems actually to feed upon orthodoxy and is more at home in a Bible Conference than in a tavern.[59]

Our faith can become about social justice. We cannot read Scripture and not be confronted about the amount of concern that Jesus has for the poor. There are over 2000 times that the Bible speaks about this.[60] To be concerned about people in their physical and financial needs is a core outworking of the Gospel. We will speak more about this in the next chapter. However, even this good thing can be distorted into the main thing. When we do this, we evaluate ourselves and others by how much they do for those in need. Over time, taking care of the ones in need and advocating for them can flow less and less from a love relationship with God, and find its energy source in our own sense of mission and image. When we do this, we use our care for the poor as a way of making ourselves feel better. If we lose the primary focus on God's intimate love and attachment, our efforts will turn angry and self-righteous and will, in the end, not amount to more than a "resounding gong or clanging cymbal" (1 Corinthians 13:1).

A depersonalized faith doesn't survive mental and emotional pain very well. Praise Jesus.

Making Jesus into someone who can only help accomplish things for earthly kingdoms places him too distant from the one who needs intimate help in pain right now. Truly, sufferers should be concerned about each of these things, but they cannot replace the primary substance of love. Paul writes,

> Therefore, be imitators of God as beloved children. And walk in love, as Christ loved us and gave himself up for us, a fragrant offering and sacrifice to God. (Ephesians 5:1-2).

The gift of suffering allows us the primacy of Christ in all things because when we suffer, he is the thing that we need. Suffering allows us the "blessedness of possessing nothing"[61]. At the same time, it lets us rest with the one who says, "Blessed are the poor in spirit, for theirs in the kingdom of God". (Matthew 5:3).

For sufferers, Christ is not a banner to raise or a cause to be fought. Christ is himself and he is free to be just him in our lives. He's enough. This communion of love cannot easily be changed back into an impersonalized system. Thanks be to God.

Treasure 5: Wounded Healing

This phrase is borrowed from Henri Nouwen, who wrote the wonderful book *The Wounded Healer*.[62] He describes Jesus this way as one who binds the wounds of the hurting, carrying their wounds into his very body. He speaks that the call of those who have received healing from Christ is to join with him as wounded healers.

A few years ago, I had the chance to have one of my favorite church experiences of all time. We took a class of over 40 people through Stephen Ministry training. Stephen Ministry is a ministry that walks towards people in need. It is a one-on-one layperson ministry that seeks to practice spiritual listening and presence to those who are in the midst of a difficult season of life. It is and remains a precious ministry in our church and in thousands of other churches internationally.

When we interviewed the people in our church who desired to become Stephen ministers, I was blown away by two things. The first thing was the depth of faith and presence of God that existed in these people. I was also deeply impacted by why they wanted to participate in the behind-the-scenes and often messy ministry. Person after person came in, describing the levels of deep pain that they had experienced in their life. They spoke of their wounds. They spoke of Christ, who had come to them in their affliction and abject need. They spoke of the sacred and informed joy of joining with him to enter the precious space of another's pain.

People who suffer mental and emotional affliction are not the only people who can serve and help heal people who are hurting. But a person who has mental and emotional suffering needs to have at least some people in their life who truly know that type of dark. People who have experienced this have a point of reference that can provide understanding, empathy and acceptance. This does not mean that all internal pain is similar or that the story of one will be the same as the other. But a person who has lived in the dark is not scared of it like those who haven't. They don't minimize it or rush someone out of it. They don't wring their hands when they are unable to fix a person's sadness. They are a non-anxious presence, a wounded healer who is able to sit and wait on God with the sufferer. They are truly the hands and feet of the great Wounded Healer himself.

There are endless treasures to be found and enjoyed with Christ. The one who has their union with Christ as the source of their life will not ignore other aspects of life but be energized to engage with it. Lewis writes,

> I believe in Christianity as I believe that the sun has risen: not only because I see it, but because by it I see everything else.[63]

In that sunlight there is great pleasure in life. There is also great freedom in the loss of things like ego, control and imperial religion. There is great gain in vulnerable fellowship, sharing sufferings with his people and serving alongside Christ as His co-wounded healers.

All of this life is a gift and the treasures found in God, when rightly ordered, are the very substance of Heaven. It is living out of the way we were taught to pray.

> Our Father in Heaven, Hallowed be your name, Your Kingdom Come Your will be done on earth as it is in Heaven. (Matthew 6:9)

<u>Prayer of the Treasure Hunters</u>

Lord, you alone are my portion and my cup;
you make my lot secure.
The boundary lines have fallen for me in pleasant places;
surely I have a delightful inheritance.
I will praise the Lord, who counsels me;
even at night my heart instructs me.
I keep my eyes always on the Lord.
With him at my right hand, I will not be shaken.
Therefore my heart is glad and my tongue rejoices; my body
also will rest secure.
Because you will not abandon me to the realm of the dead,
nor will you let your faithful one see decay.
You make known to me the path of life;
you will fill me with joy in your presence,
with eternal pleasures at your right hand.

Psalm 16:5-11

56 Mangold, James. *Indiana Jones and the Dial of Destiny.* [Film]. Walt Disney Pictures Lucasfilm Ltd. Released May 18, 2023.

57 Peterson, Eugene. *Living the Resurrection: The Risen Christ in Everyday Life.* Colorado Springs, CO: Nav Press, 2020.

58 Lewis, C.S. *The Problem of Pain.* (San Francisco: Harper One, 2015)

59 Tozer, A.W. *The Pursuit of God.* (Harrisburg, PA: Christian Publications, 1948)

60 A wonderful list of these passages can be found at https://sojo.net/list-some-more-2000verses-scripture-poverty-and-justice

61 Tozer, A.W. *The Pursuit of God.* (Harrisburg, PA: Christian Publications, 1948)

62 Nouwen, Henri. *The Wounded Healer: Ministry in Contemporary Society.* (Cincinnati, OH: Franciscan Media, 2010)

63 This quote from Lewis comes from a paper that he gave *The Oxford Socratic Club* entitled, *Is Theology Poetry?*

7

SPIRITUAL

DISPOSITIONS OF THE

AFFLICTED

The nature of this chapter is less focused on specific activities to engage in or to schedule. These are ways of the afflicted heart that are lived out with continued resolve. They are dispositions and commitments of those who experience mental and emotional suffering; they are internal ways of operating, not something to cross off on the to-do list on any given day.

Suffering does not bring about growth on its own. Without the commitment to trust Christ with the suffering, mental and emotional affliction may be the very tool that destroys that relationship. I have more respect than most for the "deconstruction" movement happening in many lives when it comes to their faith. Perhaps that is because as long as I have known Jesus, I have been in deconstruction and reconstruction mode. A lot of the reason people are deconstructing from their faith is because their faith was not personal. It was a system of beliefs that they adopted or had pushed on them. Deconstruction of that type of faith is vital. So is the reconstruction of faith and trust in a personal God through Jesus Christ. Suffering can have great deconstructive and reconstructive power, but it takes staying with Christ and his church to build an intentional new and living way.

The following are seven dispositions of how to seek and find the heart of Christ in the midst of suffering. They are basic building materials of reconstruction after suffering has done its dismantling work.

1. Awareness of the Prison of Blame

More than any other threat to the sufferer, blame can destroy a person who is suffering. It can turn suffering into eternal damage more than eternal life and union with God.

For each of us who suffer from internal affliction, we want to know whose fault it is. If we don't point a finger at the source of the problem, how can we ever dry up that stream of pain? Some of these reasons are natural and healthy. Our family systems, societal inequities and personal relationships have tremendous impacts on our mental and emotional well-being. To avoid that recognition or to tacitly say, "all is forgiven and in the past" is to greatly underestimate how much past trauma impacts everyday life. When we are able to recognize our own experiences with abuse and trauma that have happened to us, we can begin to work through them with wisdom and clarity. Understanding the cause of internal suffering, especially when it is directly from someone's action or neglect, needs the process of time, anger and grief. We cannot come to true forgiveness without an awareness of what we are forgiving in people or ourselves.

Having said that, it is so attractive to get lost in a concreted disposition of blame toward the people who caused us pain. In this way, we are guaranteeing that the pain that they caused will never find healing or hope. It is at this time that we can pass the pain forward. When we are preoccupied with the one who has wronged us, we are most susceptible to rationalize the pain that we cause to other people. If we do hurt others, we lay the blame at the feet of our perpetrator who started it all. The heart can grow so hard when set in this way. It can also create generational trauma and abuse until the cycle is changed.

Part of the temptation towards blame is that it feels a lot stronger to be mad than it does to be sad. Being hurt by someone, by definition, hurts. No one wants to feel that. If we can turn our hurt into anger, we feel tough. Anger is not wrong to feel, but it can become a drug that our pain uses to escape the vulnerable places of hurt and sadness. When we do that, we can lose seasons of our lives to the remarkable seduction of bitterness.

When the Bible teaches forgiveness in Christ, it talks about how he "once for all" completed that act of forgiveness. Because of that, we assume that's how we are supposed to pull off forgiveness, too. However, for most of us it does not functionally work like that. Forgiveness, for most of us, is not:

"I forgive you for all time and am freed from any frustration or blame that I have for what you have done by your action or neglect."

The reality of forgiving someone who caused great pain of any type sounds more like,

"I seek to forgive you today. I am going to try tomorrow, too. My goal in Christ is not just to say that I forgive you. It is to say I forgive you again and again."

Bitterness is imprisonment. There is no freedom for the person who is always talking about how someone else caused their life sentence. It is an endless prison where we can lose all sight of what God might have for us if we are unwilling to look away - in time and with the wise process - from the person who has caused it.

We must also look within. For many of us who struggle internally, we carry a large weight of self-rejection. Nouwen writes,

> Over the years, I have come to realize that the greatest trap in our lives is not success, popularity, or power but self-rejection. Success, popularity, and power can indeed present a great temptation, but their seductive quality often comes from the way they are part of the much larger temptation to self-rejection. When we have come to believe in the voices that call us worthless and unlovable, then success, popularity, and power are easily perceived as attractive solutions. The real trap, however, is self-rejection. . . . As soon as someone accuses me or

criticizes me, as soon as I am rejected, left alone, or abandoned, I find myself thinking, "Well, that proves once again that I am a nobody." . . . My dark side says, "I am no good. . . . I deserve to be pushed aside, forgotten, rejected, and abandoned."

Self-rejection is the greatest enemy of the spiritual life because it contradicts the sacred voice that calls us the "Beloved." Being the Beloved constitutes the core truth of our existence.[64]

Self-rejection will mobilize us to try all kinds of external efforts so that we can finally accept and not reject ourselves. If we are not able to accept the love of God in Jesus Christ, the true forgiveness of our sins and turn towards the freedom of acceptance and compassion towards ourselves, we simply cannot grow from suffering.

To be lost in blame is to be lost. It is to go to reckless war with ourselves or with another. The tools of blame are weapons of mass destruction, causing radiating devastation that can last an entire life. The tools of healing are careful, conscious of complexity, and gentle. They are not absent from big feelings, angry outbursts and deep wounds. But, in the hands of the Master Physician, they also do not lose sight of love.

Dear person who struggles with internal affliction, do not flee compassion even when you are angry, even when you wisely understand who has caused your pain and loss. If you lose sight of compassion, you will lose the ability to experience God in your suffering. Then, it is just a spiral of pain without purpose. Blame that cannot come to compassion will rob you of a healing union with Christ himself. It is the number one prison of the internally afflicted.

2. Wonder

I had a close friend ask me an insightful question when I was going through a difficult season with anxiety. He asked me, "Ben, what is your wonder life like?"

That's it. He didn't try to make it sound less weird.

He did thankfully clarify what he meant because, on the first pass, it sounded like some alternate universe internet game in which I was able to create my own reality. By the way, I would fly, be a talented musician and be a starting safety on the Philadelphia Eagles. But that's not what he meant.

He asked me because he found that getting outside of his own head was really important for him. He found that when he was taken back by the wonder of God, which he did not cause nor could stop, he was included in something bigger than himself; someone bigger than himself. This was bigger than the worries, stresses and oft soul-deadening monotonous work of the day.

He also shared with me how wonder operates in the life of the internally afflicted.

Wonder is not about reduction. That's not how wonder works. It does not diminish the size and scope of who we are or what we face. It does not minimize or scorn the amount of pain that exists in the sufferer. It's a gift to the wounded one is not to stop or shrink pain.

Wonder is also not about expansion. It does not inflate us or pep-talk us into thinking that we are bigger or even equal to the thing in front of us. Wonder is not a peppy trainer telling us that we can indeed lift that which we thought we couldn't. In the darkness of significant suffering, usually, we can't.

Wonder doesn't shrink suffering or expand our own strength to conquer it.

Wonder is about something outside of both our suffering and our resources to defeat it.

Wonder is about reality. Wonder is the realization that there really is One whose scope is far beyond all else.

Yes, all else.

There is One who is bigger than all the accumulated suffering of person and creation, beyond all the evil and systemic oppression that exists, beyond all the days and nights of complicated and significant mental and emotional pain.

Wonder is being reminded of the grandeur of God and the things he has constructed. Things that are not destroyed or broken by all that ails us, no matter how overwhelming it is, how long it lingers and how much it hurts.

Wonder doesn't deny suffering. Wonder gives us something to see that is bigger and beyond it.

I can't tell you how much I love being near the water. I love lakes, oceans, streams and anything that shows the wonder of God in water. It is powerful, expansive and contains so much life. For me, it is important - when I am in a difficult season with internal pain - to get around the wonder that I feel when I am around water. It pulls me out of my own circumstances into a world that I did not make, cannot improve and won't easily ruin. The stakes are off. God is in charge of the beautiful landscape and ecosystem of water. I can just watch and enjoy.

Thomas Merton concluded his book, *The New Seeds of Christian Contemplation,* with these words. Beware: they are a lot to chew on, but I have come to deeply believe in the truth of wonder of which he speaks.

> What is serious to men is often very trivial in the sight of God. What in God might appear to us as "play" is perhaps what he Himself takes most seriously. At any rate, the Lord plays and diverts Himself in the garden of His creation, and if we could let go of our own obsession with what we think is the meaning of it all, we might be able to hear His call and follow Him in His mysterious, cosmic dance. We do not have to go very far to catch echoes of that game and of that dancing. When we are alone on a starlit night; when by chance we see the migrating birds in autumn descending on a grove of junipers to rest and eat; when we see children in a moment when they are really children; when we know love in our own hearts; or when, like the Japanese poet Bashō we hear an old frog land in a quiet pond with a solitary splash--at such times the awakening, the turning inside out of all values, the "newness," the emptiness and the purity of vision that make themselves evident, provide a glimpse of the cosmic dance.

> For the world and time are the dance of the Lord in emptiness. The silence of the spheres is the music of a wedding feast. The more we persist in misunderstanding the phenomena of life, the more we analyze them into

strange finalities and complex purposes of our own, and the more we involve ourselves in sadness, absurdity and despair. But it does not matter much because no despair of ours can alter the reality of things or stain the joy of the cosmic dance that is always there. Indeed, we are in the midst of it, and it is in the midst of us, for it beats in our very blood, whether we want it to or not.

Yet the fact remains that we are invited to forget ourselves on purpose, cast our awful solemnity to the winds and join in the general dance.[65]

When was the last time that you were caught up in wonder? Who are the people that help you build your "wonder life"? Where are physical places that are near you that help you get lost in God's creation? These are the places where Heaven and Earth blur their lines. What type of art helps you get out of your own head and helps you have a disposition of awe? It is of such import to find the things and spaces that help us see the seriousness of the bigness of our world and the One who has made and continues to sustain it.

3. Connection to the poor

We mentioned in the last chapter that there are 2000 Bible verses talking about the care of the poor.[66] That's a lot. Dealing with mental and emotional suffering is its own type of poverty. But, it is also confusing to know how to talk about or describe. It is also one that changes in different life seasons. There is something special about knowing a God who loves the physically and financially poor for someone who struggles with a less tangible need.

This is true for a few reasons. 1) It is the call of all Christians to be mindful of the poor, regardless of internal status or felt health. When we are near the poor, we are nearer to Christ himself.

> For I was hungry and you gave me food, I was thirsty and you gave me drink, I was a stranger and you welcomed me, I was naked and you clothed me, I was sick and you visited me, I was in prison and you came to me.' Then the righteous will answer him, saying, 'Lord, when did we see you hungry and feed you, or thirsty and give you drink? And when did we see you a stranger and welcome you, or naked and clothe you? And when did we see you sick or in prison and visit you?' And the King will answer them, 'Truly, I say to you, as you did it to one of the least of these my brothers, you did it to me.' (Matthew 25:35-40)

2) Dealing with the poor takes away the sense that there are easy solutions to complex problems. This is such an identification point for those who struggle internally.

3) It is often where wounded healers find that they can truly listen and make a small impact without condescension.

Some of us live in wealthy and others in poor areas. Our networks, churches and social fabric may or may not easily include living life frequently with those who do not have many earthly resources. However, in every place in the world, there are the poor among us. Often, in the greatest places of wealth, those serving the wealthy are in very difficult circumstances. Christ promised, "For the poor, you always have with you" (John 12:8), and their needs are not as far as we might want to pretend.

If you have substantial means or income, you are part of an externally privileged group of people. If you struggle with emotional and mental pain, you are a part of an impoverished internal group of people. This places you in a very unique and profound position to help connect the communities of those with resources and those without. You understand more than many people with resources what it's like to feel desperate or alone. You not only have the chance to grow deeply from your connection to those without resources but are uniquely positioned to have a profound impact on networking.

4) Lastly, living life in the presence of or at least in the awareness of the needs of the poor places you with a special community. There is a great need for love here but less of a need to be impressive. That is such a welcome change from so many of our insecure environments.

4. Hospitality toward yourself

We are called to love ourselves. I know that sounds so dissonant to what you may have heard in your faith journey. But, it is true. It is a part of our worship of God to value what he values, which includes ourselves.

> And one of the scribes came up and heard them disputing with one another and, seeing that he answered them well, asked him, "Which commandment is the most

important of all?" Jesus answered, "The most important is, 'Hear, O Israel: The Lord our God, the Lord is one. And you shall love the Lord your God with all your heart and with all your soul and with all your mind and with all your strength.' The second is this: 'You shall love your neighbor as yourself.' There is no other commandment greater than these." (Mark 12:28-34).

Jesus says there is a hierarchy of loves. These loves make up the greatest responsibilities of the human. They order the way the human is designed to function now and forever. First, love God above all else. Second, Love your neighbor as yourself. Loving yourself is an implied part of this call. If we do not love ourselves than we could not fulfill the second most important command in Scripture. Jesus assumes that our love should be for ourselves because he made us operate this way. He does not ask for our love for others to go beyond our love of self but calls us to the sacrificial and important call of loving both.

Anyone who has tried to live a life that only loves God and others quickly realizes that they are still trying to love themselves by using those other loves; they try to prove to themself that they are good and lovable. It is deep in all of us to want to care for ourselves. What we do with that can be cruel, selfish and myopic. But the call to care for ourselves is as important as the call to love our neighbor.

The true self that is made in God's image reflects him and his nature[67]. It is unique and valuable. It needs to be discovered, understood and nurtured in Christ. This true self is worthy, designed and redeemed by God himself. And it must be hosted well. The problem is for many of us, we simply are not kind hosts to ourselves.

Recently, my wife and I took a trip to Colombia, where her sister lives. She is a clever host. She asked me one day, "What Colombian food do you like the most?" as a way of making conversation. We were staying at her house, and guess what showed up at lunch the next day? The exact thing that I mentioned in answer to her question. She was looking at my needs, seeking to understand what I enjoyed and how I would feel loved.

This hospitable disposition towards ourselves is vital. It is so easy for us who struggle with mental and emotional difficulty to simply despise our sensitivity or our struggle. When we operate towards our own needs this way, we are not agents of healing, compassion or love for ourselves. Being a good host towards our own legitimate needs and limits, is to know ourselves and to care for ourselves as well. I recognize this sounds like selfishness, and I can hear the old camp song in my head: "I don't want to be a selfishly, swimming along singing my song...". But what I am talking about is not sin. It is holiness. It honors the God who loves you by treating you well that which he has determined to be of great value.

"Self-care" has gotten a bad rep partially because it is used to justify sitting in bed all day with beer and Netflix. But true self care, the self care that God has made us do, is to see, know, nurture, protect and host our very selves with the loving kindness of God.

Nouwen, who writes on this interior concept of home/ hospitality more than any author that I am aware of, writes,

> Home is the center of my being where I can hear the voice that says: 'You are my Beloved, on you my favor rests' - the same voice that gave life to the first Adam and spoke to Jesus, the second Adam; the same voice that speaks to all the children of God and sets them free to live in the midst of a dark world while remaining in the light.[68]

To live in this central, familiar home in our lives, we must become people of compassion and gentleness. This is true in how we welcome Christ. This is true in how we welcome the other. None of those will remain compassionate and gentle, however, if we do not welcome ourselves.

I have found over and over in my interactions with people as a pastor that those who have a kind and compassionate disposition toward their true selves also reflect that in their disposition toward people around them. Those who are full of judgement and harshness within will inevitably reflect that to those who are close to them.

5. Wisdom when to distrust your own thinking and feeling

When we are in physical pain, we have trouble with our motor skills. It's hard to thread a needle after stubbing your toe. When that pain is internal, our emotional and mental worlds become preoccupied with pain, too. We are close to our fight and flight systems. We have trouble remaining centered, hopeful, calm and making all of the right decisions. Many people who struggle with mental and emotional wellness have trouble with addictive substances and behaviors because this is a way to get away from the pain. As one person told me, "I don't do drugs to feel something. I do them to stop feeling something". The consequences of those decisions are not deeply thought through. The survival system demands relief and safety and we are susceptible to give it whatever it is asking for, whether it is healthy or not.

I find that when I am struggling internally, everything feels like a potential catastrophe. It becomes difficult to know what is a true threat and what is imagined. During seasons of depression, my view of myself is also very distorted. It becomes difficult to know who I am, where I am going and why I should even remain here.

One of the loneliest feelings that I have as a struggler is the healthy realization that there are times when I can't trust my own mind. It's really painful to not be able to trust your mind.

Here are some things to say to ourselves when we are having trouble finding our footing.

"I have trouble knowing what is real right now. But, when I was more at peace, this is what I believed, so I am going to stick with that. Lord, have mercy."

"I am going to reach out right now because those who know and love me know when I have trouble seeing straight. They are not thrown by my anxious thinking and can be a place of mooring for me in the storm. I have learned who to trust when I can't trust me very much. Lord, have mercy."

"I honestly do not know what to do, think or feel and I have to trust that is okay for now. Lord, have mercy."

"I need not to be a slave to all the impulses of relief that come from desperation. Lord, have mercy."

"I'm not okay and I don't know the solution to this problem or episode. But, I am fully, deeply loved by God and that matters more than the mental stability that I crave. Lord, have mercy."

6. Christ-like Rhythm: "Ruthlessly Eliminate Hurry from your life"

This is a quote from Dallas Willard from a conversation he had with John Ortberg. Ortberg writes about it in his book, *Soul Keeping*.

> Entering into a very busy season of ministry, I called Dallas to ask him what I needed to do to stay spiritually healthy. I pictured him sitting in that room as we talked. There was a long pause - with Dallas, there was nearly always a long pause - and then he said slowly, "You must ruthlessly eliminate hurry from your life." I quickly wrote that down. Most people take notes with Dallas; I have even seen his wife take notes, which my wife rarely does with me.
>
> "Okay, Dallas," I responded. "I've got that one. Now, what other spiritual nuggets do you have for me? I don't have a lot of time, and I want to get all the spiritual wisdom from that I can."
>
> "There is nothing else," he said, enormously acting as if he did not notice my impatience. "Hurry is the great enemy of the spiritual life in our day. You must

ruthlessly eliminate hurry from you life."[69]

I don't think there is a single quote that is repeated in modern spiritual formation literature more than this one. It is a simple statement attributed to a brilliant man. The thing I find remarkable is that there are so many spiritual teachers who agree with this sentiment that hurry is the great enemy of nurturing a heart at peace with God. This story and some other Dallas Willard statements on hurry are found frequently in sermons, books, and pastoral meetings.

The pace and rhythm of God is much slower than how most of us live our lives. When I am able to spend deep time with God, I can feel my whole being, including my pulse, actually slow down.

When we are experiencing mental or emotional suffering, the felt need is to get out at all costs. When that is not an option that we are able to have, we can then stuff our lives full with as much distraction, service and busyness as possible. It is as if we say, "If I keep rushing around, then I can avoid the pain that I am feeling". We each know this leads to only more running, which leads to exhaustion and breakdown. Even as I write this, I am taken aback by my own hypocrisy. I have lived that cycle more times than I want to admit. I have lived it as a husband, father, pastor and friend. My wife can actually see it in my eyes when I live in this type of urgency. She affectionately says, "You have your crazy eyes". Hurried life makes crazy eyes, ones that do not see the loving gaze of the Father well at all. Kierkegaard was credited with a statement from his journal,

"The result of busyness is that the individual is very

seldom permitted to form a heart."[70]

Learning to live within a wise rhythm of life is foundational for those of us who struggle with internal pain. We naturally are not able to move as fast as some of our more light-hearted friends. That is okay. Some people are able to accomplish things on a straight-away highway at higher speeds. Those things are often done more superficially but I suppose that could be okay at times, too. I have come to see my inner road has a lot of twists and turns and treacherous places. If I try to speed through them, I am guaranteed a crash. Hurry is the enemy of the soul and a perilous risk for those who struggle with interior pain.

Conversely, learning to live within our own limitations is a necessary and Godly thing. Kelly Kapic writes,

> God is the good Creator who designed us as good creatures. Part of the good of being a creature is having limits. The incarnation is God's great yes to his creation, including human limits. God designed the person for the community and the community for the person. The Creator is also the Sustainer and Redeemer. We are never asked to relate to God in any way other than as humans.[71]

7. Focusing small: Just the next step

The Scripture teaches us that suffering is a part of the walk of a Christian life. That suffering has many intended purposes and what can be accomplished cannot be replaced.

But, the hard part of long-term suffering is it is just exhausting. For those who struggle with interior pain, you know that it just gets so old after a while. It is heavy to live today and overwhelming to think of this potentially being there for the rest of life.

While it is so important to find God in the pain, seek the treasures that are found at his right hand and steward our crosses well, there are days when those things sound a million miles away. It feels like the weight of interior pain is unspiritual and only demoralizing.

For many who struggle with depression, the depression is less violent, as David describes and more dull and blank. It feels so far from having any possible virtue or lesson within it. The felt desire is simply to just go back to bed.

There are many days when all the ideas presented in this book are too big to hold on to. There are days that are not made for strategy and deep process. There are days when the greatest thing you can do is to simply keep going. It is simply to make your next meeting, eat your next meal, parent the next need of your child or turn in your next assignment. There are days that cannot contain the weight of processing all of your feelings and thoughts about them. Those days, we need simply to take the next step.

Life is beautiful and your life is a gift. It does not always feel that way and interior pain translates life into some dark interpretations. Keep going.

There are days that feel like you have been tortured for hours with no point at all, no conclusions at all, no beautiful aha moments at all. Keep going.

There are times that God seems to be absent, lost in a gray of pain and confusion. Your prayers barely make it out of your mouth and feel like they don't get as far as your bedroom ceiling. Keep going.

There are moments when you wonder if you are making up the fact that God could use this type of suffering. You don't need to prove to yourself that he will or try to convince all of your emotions that he is coming soon to make sense of it all. Just live now. Keep going.

For those struggling with emotional and mental affliction, the bravest thing that you can do, the greatest defiance towards darkness that you can make, is not trying to shine a great light or give a passionate rally cry. It is to keep going. Just keep going.

Mental and emotional pain can be very disorienting. It is important to cultivate healthy dispositions in our lives because when the enemy attacks it is a hard time to repair the walls of the city. We need daily commitment to building godly strength to weather what comes our way and to build pathways of redemption that can be an anchor in the storm.

Prayer for the Dispositions of Productive Suffering

Father,

You are not stressed today. You have no anxious thoughts. When you look into the parts of my life, you do not wring your hands in angst or confusion. You are whole, safe and exist in an eternal communion of love that drives out fear.

Help me, my Father. Please.

Help me cultivate inner dispositions that lead me towards that kingdom of love. Help me participate with my co-worker, brother and Lord - Jesus. Help me one step at a time to make pathways of peace in the midst of pain, trails of quietness in the midst of my internal noise and habits of rhythm in what feels like chaos.

On this day, help my "normal" way to be shifted slightly, slowly and thoroughly. Invite me deeper into Your pathways of suffering, not for suffering sake, but suffering so that I might be closer to you, your family and myself. Grant me the grace to learn to walk in these ways of faith, hope and love. Here in that place, even in the midst of suffering, all is made well.

---

[64] Nouwen, Henri J.M. *Life of the Beloved: Spiritual Living in a Secular World.* (Crossroads Publishing, 2002)

[65] Merton, Thomas. *New Seeds of Contemplation.* (New York, NY, New Directions Publishing, 1972).

[66] It is worth going to the following site to read through the passages listed. About 10 years ago, I began to realize that my Bible spoke about the needs of the poor much more than I did. The shear amount of Scripture about this is worth reading through. https://sojo.net/list-some-more-2000verses-scripture-poverty-and-justice

[67] There has been great work written about the "true self" and the "false self". It is very helpful language as many in the church have translated the self as only a construct of sin. However, we are uniquely made in God's image and the more we grow into Christ, the more we become our truest selves. There are many who have spent a long time on this subject. A wonderful introductory work to this subject is the following.

Benner, David. *The Gift of Being Yourself; The Sacred Call to Self-Discovery.* (Downers Grove, IL: Intervarsity Press, 2015).

[68] Nouwen, Henri. *Return of the Prodigal Son: A Story of Homecoming.* New York, NY, 1994).

[69] Ortberg, John. *Soul Keeping: Caring for the Most Important Part of You.* (Grand Rapids, MI: Zondervan, 2014).

[70] Kapic, Kelly. "Take Time to be Unproductive: How Busyness can Waste A Life." *Desiring God Articles.* July 28, 2022. https://www.desiringgod.org/articles/take-time-to-be-unproductive

[71] Kapic, Kelly M. *You're Only Human; How Your Limits Reflect God's Design and Why That's Good News.* (Grand Rapids, MI: Brazos Press, 2022)

8

SPIRITUAL PRACTICES

OF THE AFFLICTED

One of the primary reasons people seek spiritual counsel is because they simply cannot find God and are not sure where to look. These questions have been on the mind of every pilgrim - How do we actually, truly experience God? How do we know if we are in his presence? How can he feel close and involved and connected to my life in everyday living? These are beautiful questions and come from hearts that do not just want to seek the hand of God in their lives, but his very face and presence near and now. For those in resilient internal pain, these questions are far from theoretical or even theological. They are questions of basic spiritual survival.

In his book, *Walking with God*, John Eldridge writes of an experience that he had talking with someone who was having trouble hearing from God. He wrote,

"It takes time," I said. "It's something we learn. Name one thing in your life that you really enjoy doing that didn't require practice to get there."

If you want to make music, you have to learn how to play an instrument. And in the beginning, it doesn't sound too good—all the squawks and squeaks and bad timing. You really are on your way to making music. It just sounds like you are strangling a pig. If you stick with it, something beautiful begins to emerge. Or how about snowboarding—learning to do that is really awkward at first. You fall down a lot. You feel like an idiot. But if you hang in there, you come to enjoy it. You get better. It starts to feel natural. That's when it becomes fun. This holds true for anything in life.

Including our walk with God. It takes time and practice. It's awkward at first, and sometimes we feel stupid. But if we hang in there, we do begin to get it, and as it becomes more and more natural, our lives are filled with his presence and all the joy, beauty and pleasure that comes with it. It is something to be learned. And it is worth learning.[72]

I feel a little guilty including this analogy, because I tried snowboarding one time, was sore for days and immediately went back to skiing. My backside clearly advocated that flying down a hill on two things was a lot easier than on one.

Snowboarding guilt aside, this analogy resonates deeply with me. In our walk with God, depth takes time. It takes practice. We do not engage in spiritual practices in order to achieve God, earn his love or gain favor. We do them to know him more. God is personal and like any relationship, it takes time and effort to engage. There are ways that we practice resurrection in our daily lives.

I am going to include a variety of practices that can be helpful for those who deal with mental and emotional anguish. This is not to take away from other practices or to be the full sum of Christian practice. This is meant to offer some helpful, often historical, ideas on how to connect to God while in pain. Please treat this as a buffet and not as a checklist. Knowing yourself and how you live and connect will mean that different ones of these practices will help different people. Also, similar to a buffet, if you try to gorge yourself on all of them, you will grow to not enjoy the food.

I would encourage you to try these practices and see what is most helpful for you and God as you connect together in the midst of mental and emotional pain.

Spend extended time with God in prayer.

The contemplatives use great language to describe how to spend extended time with God. They encourage time in prayer that has no "scaffolding" or extra devices that we would normally use to help us get spiritual. This means spending extended time with God without your favorite worship songs. It means taking time to listen and speak with him without getting pumped up by your favorite author or spiritual podcast. It means taking hours - I would suggest starting with 3 - with God alone.

Just you. Just him.

What normally happens during times like this is a lot of confusion and frustration. God feels a little less awesome and close. All of the sudden, it feels like a lot of silence.

Lean in.

Let your attachments to feeling spiritual fall away. Keep listening. Keep telling him how weird you feel about trying to fill this time. Tell him you think I was dumb for suggesting doing this. Just stay in there.

Just you. Just him.

I received training from a wonderful community of people at The Leadership Institute. They are "An International Discipling Community", and their intention is to "inspire generations of leaders to listen to God, follow Jesus' rhythms of life and lead from the overflow".[73]

In each of their retreats, they had us take this extended time with God. No lengthy instruction. No scaffolding. And then we spent the next session talking about what we experienced. Did he talk? Why do you think that he did/didn't? What did you learn? What was frustrating or ego striking? How did he show himself to you and what did he say? The first time we did this, I simply wrote down words people were saying about their time with God and what they experienced with him. At the end I had a word bank of what the participants said. I remember looking at all the descriptions and feeling the simple but overwhelming feeling, these words describe the One I love. Being with people who had been with God for this experience was such a treasure to me. We had different backgrounds and undoubtedly separate life experiences and convictions about things. But these people were my people, because we spoke a language of soul taught to us by the practice of prayer.

It was a language of him. Just him.

He speaks. He really does. It is often clunky and hard to listen. It is hard to become quiet. Doubts and frustration are part of the process. But the practice of extended time plays an important role in stripping us away from the loudness of the agendas of our day. Those who struggle with a lot of internal pain have a lot of internal noise. That takes time to wade in and find some quiet for God to be easily heard. Our souls themselves take time to come out. Parker Palmer writes,

The soul is like a wild animal—tough, resilient, savvy, self-sufficient and yet exceedingly shy. If we want to see a wild animal, the last thing we should do is to go crashing through the woods, shouting for the creature to come out. But if we are willing to walk quietly into the woods and sit silently for an hour or two at the base of a tree, the creature we are waiting for may well emerge, and out of the corner of an eye, we will catch a glimpse of the precious wildness we seek.[74]

Intentional Meetings

In most churches, announcements often go like this: "Please come to this event/ministry because it is going to be fun and you are going to have fellowship with people in your life stage". I am not trying to be snarky here, and I do believe a great reason to go to a church event is to get to know people in the body of Christ.

However, it becomes easy to allow our ministries to almost

always target "fun and fellowship" because a lack of connection with people is almost always a felt need in the people we serve.

Here is my encouragement: find the meeting that your church does that has —as its primary goal— connecting and communicating with God. The importance of community is paramount. But, the community found with God as its true source, not its tacit one, is of primary importance. It may be a prayer meeting with senior saints. It may be a spiritually vibrant Bible study that is not well attended. It may be with an addiction group that meets in the church basement. It doesn't matter. Find where God is and go there. This does not mean not being involved in other ministries or looking down on them, but if you want to grow in your relationship with God, get as close to the epicenter as possible. Be with the people who want the epicenter the most. My concern is that if we are always trying to scratch the consumer crowd itch who want more friends, we are losing the people who have come to church to truly, deeply work on their relationship with God himself. Find the ministry or meeting where he is most purely the goal, and prioritize it.

When we are going through emotional and mental pain, we need substance. When establishing relationships with fellow pilgrims who truly know him, you begin to deepen with him with them. If they are older than you, more married than you, more or less in style than you, even if they suffer less than you do, make the people who really know him your people. When he is the center, all things will find their place.

"Christ with Us" Prayer exercise

The majority of the time that we pray is in the name of Jesus and to the person of the Father. Of course, this changes and there is not a wrong part of the Godhead to talk to. In this prayer exercise, we pray to Jesus.

This is an exercise based on something I have heard called the Immanuel Prayer.[75] I have modified the process to try to fit it closely to the invitation of Christ found in Hebrews 4:14-16.

It is a prayer exercise that is based on his compassion meeting us right where we are.

Since then, we have a great high priest who has passed through the heavens, Jesus, the Son of God, let us hold fast our confession. For we do not have a high priest who is unable to sympathize with our weaknesses, but one who in every respect has been tempted as we are, yet without sin. Let us then with confidence draw near to the throne of grace, that we may receive mercy and find grace to help in time of need. (Hebrews 4:14-16)

Here are the steps to the prayer:
1. "You saw me getting here."
Review your day. What were the parts of today that you remember. Consciously recall that he saw each part and remembers it better than you do.

Write your prayers: "You saw me when I thought _____", "You saw me when I felt _____", "You saw me when I experienced _____".

2. "You see me sitting here."

(What is happening in your physical world? Where are you? What are you feeling in your body? What are you doing? What are you distracted by? What do you see and sense in your environment?)

Write your prayers: "You see that my knees hurt right now because of ... You see that I am full after a great lunch ..." You see that I am tired because the game went late last night.")

3. "You see my thinking, processing and feeling just as I am."

(What are you feeling ... without muting or rationalizing? What do you want ... what desire is strong in you this day? What are you worried about? What are you excited about? What is capturing your mind and your attention? What details of your day are on repeat in your mind?)

Write your prayers: "You see that I feel _____ because of _____". Take time with this step to really process.

4. "You see this with compassion."

(How does Christ view my realities with compassion?)

Go over the things that you have just written. The happy stuff. The frustrated stuff. The stuff in between. Realize that as you have experienced those things and are experiencing these things, he sees those everyday thoughts and experiences with compassion.

Write your prayers: "You see me with compassion and you feel with me as I am experiencing _____."

5. "You can help."

How can the compassionate Christ give you strength, help and mercy in the time of your need? As you look at the list you have made above and realize what has worried or excited you, how can Christ engage there?

Write your prayers: "You can help as I face or feel this situation. You can help as I enter this specific confusion, pain, need, hope etc."

Your written words will have a lot of the same sentences in them. But, as you write out what you have experienced, are experiencing and where you need help, you can slowly sense his presence in all things.

Meditative Reading of Scripture

This is an exercise of a prayerful and slow way of reading and listening to God in Scripture.[76] It is one that has meant much to me in my personal life and marriage. The exercise includes the thoughtful reading of Scripture, sitting in silence, and listening if God chooses to speak directly through His Word.

A great way to begin doing this is to spend time in the Gospels, although this can be used across the landscape of Scripture. You could choose the next passage in Scripture in the book of the Bible that you are reading. Choose a complete passage or story, as short as the text allows. This usually ends up being a few verses or more. If you are in a large teaching like the Sermon on the Mount, choose a part of the teaching, like the beatitudes or the teaching on anger.

1. <u>Pray and welcome God and yourself to this time.</u>

Settle your heart and take a quick inventory. When my wife and I do this together, we ask each other to "check-in". This usually means picking a couple of words that describe how we are feeling in the moment and then sharing why. We allow our feelings to be what they are. Without edit. Without excuse. We sometimes check in as apathetic or overwhelmed, angry or at peace, scared or feeling safe, stressed or sleepy. Almost always, we find that we are a mix of a couple of things. It's important whether you are doing this with someone or with yourself, to not judge what you are feeling as you check in. It is a violation to communicate in any way that what the other person is experiencing is unacceptable. For example, if you or someone else is saying, "I am angry about work, stressed at home and fearful God doesn't love me", there is one response: "Thank you".

In this way, we welcome each other or ourselves as we are without trying to edit out part of what we are feeling. We also can welcome Christ as he is. One of my favorite questions to ask God is simply, "What are you experiencing today?" This usually leads me more to holy imagination than him directly responding, but it is important for me to remember that God came to be himself, too.

2. <u>Read the passage slowly.</u>

On the first reading, just absorb the text. If you are a Bible expert and you know this passage by heart, try to hear it anew again. Let the Scripture hit you as it was like the first time you have read it.

Spend some time in silence, chewing over what you just read. Think about what struck you the most in the reading. The chances are that you don't remember each part of the teaching or every twist in the story. But isolate one thing that stands out to you. It could be a word that was used often. It could be a detail in the story that seemed surprising or confusing to you.

If you are doing this with someone else, at the end of the silence, share with the other person what stood out to you and why.

3. Read the same passage slowly a second time.

You may want to read the passage in a different translation or may find it helpful to read the exact version over again. This time, as you are reading, take yourself into the text. If it's a story, picture yourself there. You can play the story audibly on your phone and close your eyes. Ask what would the weather have been like? What are the primary characters in the story likely feeling? What are the extra characters in the story experiencing?

If the passage is a teaching, ask yourself, what would this be like to hear for the first time? What would it be like for this teacher to teach it? How would the first hearers of these words react to this?

It is usually easier to find an emotive word to describe how you experience the text as you enter it. Sometimes I feel confused or frustrated. Sometimes, I feel free and so relieved. Sometimes, I feel so thankful and other times, I am a little scared. But, allow yourself to be there and to take the teachings and stories as they are.

Sit in silence with this. Picture the time of day you think this happened, or imagine where you were sitting if you heard this teaching from Christ or this teacher in the 1st century.

Share your words or emotions that you experience from this story or teaching. When doing this with one another, this is such a precious experience. People identify and see the same beautiful words from different perspectives and vantage points. It is fascinating and beautiful to share your thoughts and to hear the reflection of other Christ-ones as they enter into this truth with you. The text becomes so alive in these moments.

4. Read the text slowly a third time.

While you have spent the last time going into the text, this is where we ask the text to come into us. Read the text with an open question to God, what do you want me to hear today?

After reading, allow a longer time of silence. Wait on the Lord. Ask him if he has something directly for you that he wants you to hear, know, change, or respond to. If he does, sit with that, wonder about that, thank him for that.

If you do not sense that he is speaking to you directly, thank him for that, too and ask what general principle or insight this passage has for your day today. Share that with another if you are doing it with them.

5. Pray and go and practice what you have received.

There is great value in the meditative reading of Scripture for someone going through mental and emotional suffering. It is so helpful for our internal culture to have to meet and adapt to the culture of Scripture. Our insides can feel so busy the times of built-in silence help us to listen. Of course, our minds will wander and we begin focusing and worrying about our own lives. In those moments, we do not need to grow angry at ourselves and shame our un-spiritual instincts. We simply welcome ourselves back. We welcome him back. We see this as another opportunity to return. The silence helps us to get out of ourselves.

The multiple readings of the passage help us descend into it. The Scripture is so rich and each text is so full, that the multiple readings give a chance to those struggling with their own pain to gaze at an eternal truth, a lasting, important story. There is something about being with God in Scripture that is expansive and much bigger than the scope of our worries. Being with him in the text, we can be brought out of our own narrow thinking and internal judgments. We are taken to a different vantage point. In these times, God can feel so big and so near at the same time.

This way of praying and reading also forces us to listen. When we are in difficult seasons, we appropriately cry out to God for help and relief. We have a lot to ask and a lot to vent. This exercise of prayerful reading gives us time to listen to what he might have to say, not just to what our own pain is feeling. Rowan Williams put it well when he simply said,

> ...you realize that Bible-reading is an essential part of the Christian life because Christian Life is a Listening Life. Christians are people who expect to be spoken to by God.[77]

Listen to Sermons Wisely

I do not write this to discredit preaching. I don't say this to communicate that God does not have specific lessons for each of us, even in some of the rougher sermons we hear. The fastest way to lose sight of God's instruction for us during preaching is for us to be proud or defended against it. Always. I am not saying listen to sermons "sort of" or "selectively". I am saying to listen to sermons wisely.

During difficult seasons of mental health, I often have to receive sermons with my own awareness of where I am coming from. I remember a sermon that I heard while being spiritually exhausted and having a very difficult time understanding God's love. I listened to a missionary preacher who gave a talk about something—I don't remember. At one point, he used an illustration of how he was able to spend hours with God in prayer. What came over me was immediate guilt. "Yikes, I haven't spent that much time in a row with God recently. I guess that's what I have to do now". It left me not hopeful but burdened and despairing because there always seemed to be a magic fix by just doing more work a little harder, and uninterrupted hours in prayer must be the next assignment. The preacher never would have asked me to interpret his message this way. If he was talking just to me, he would have talked in a different way and approached me differently. This is not the preacher's fault that I took his words and beset myself with them. It was what I brought to the sermon. I added my guilt and pain to his words and influenced their meaning, like dumping a half a cup of salt on a fried egg. Yes, the egg may still be an egg but it is digested far differently when influenced with that much extra seasoning.

When we listen to sermons, we need to understand where we are coming from and through what lens we are listening. Otherwise, we are going to hear and apply the wrong thing out of a potentially true and well-intended message.

If you struggle with anxiety, know that you are going to find reasons to worry about whether or not you are doing it right. Strong preaching that calls you to question yourself may make you go bananas much more than help you learn from the Holy Spirit. Don't take it "from the Lord" to over-examine if he is not specifically inviting you to do so. Many preachers are trying to reach the spiritual deaf and speak so loudly that it bursts the eardrum of the overly self-conscious.

If you struggle with grief over the loss of a loved one, know you are going to experience unintentional hurt from preachers giving examples about their family or friends. They are not wrong to use an example and they are not trying to rub it in that you have lost your friends, child, spouse, etc. They may have assumed incorrectly that their connected life experience are shared by all, and the words meant to make a different point were used to pang your places of loneliness and loss.

There are also times when preachers think that their insides are like everyone else's. I suppose we all do that. I recently heard a preacher talking about how he bursts out to bed in the morning with excitement, knowing that the Lord has good things in store for that day. While I agree with the good God can do in a day, it is not my normal experience to throw off the covers in elation that another morning has come.

There are times when a preacher does not have awareness or consciousness about interior pain and speaks about it as if they do. When this happens, we have to be careful not to over accept the message or use it as a platform of bitterness. It is hard to hear careless sermons about joy that don't take darkness into account. It is hard to hear quips about depression or mocking statements about the "myth of mental health" or calling psychology "psychobabble" when someone does not really understand the depths with which those things have been helpful in identifying your own pain and story. But it remains very important to not judge preachers too harshly that say triggering things. They are on a journey like everyone and will overstate and understate things in a way that will cause pain. It is a very difficult task to challenge sin and comfort sadness at the same time.

I believe that this is also why the Lord often allows preachers to experience both deep forgiveness and profound sorrow in their lives. Their lives can tell of the freedom of deliverance and also the pain of stuck sorrow. Meetings amongst pastors are often deep and raw because pain is a language that most have come to know as a pastor and as a person. Very few pastors that I know do not have a lot of luggage with them from the land of hardship. I know this is a grace, but there are some times when I have gotten with pastors that feel really sad, too. It does not excuse preachers who unnecessarily hurt people, but it is a reminder that our own hurts can interpret things in a way that they may not have meant.

Therapy

It is possible that the holiest thing that you can do in your life today is to call a Christian therapist. There are people in your life you wish would read that sentence. And it's a heck of a lot easier to want someone else to read it than to admit that it could be meant for ourselves.

I know that my wife will laugh when she reads this. This is because I am writing to myself here, too. I have a really hard time reaching out for counseling help when I need it.

I feel defeated picking up my phone and calling a therapist, even though I have needed to do it fairly often in my life. I feel sad and at a loss when I do so. I feel like I am flashing the bat signal that I need help and can't beat the bad guys on my own. I want to be Batman - the one who figures out the problem and defeats it heroically. I do not want to be the guy who turns on the light on the roof for someone else to come and save the day. The bat signal is cool for Batman. But it's not necessarily a good feeling for those calling for help.

Here is the deal, though. Many, if not most, of us need counseling. I am blessed to be in a pastoral and staff community that celebrates, supports and encourages each other to go to counseling. It very well may be because most of us know that we need it and so celebrating it with the other pastors and ministry leaders makes us feel better about receiving it ourselves.

I have advocated here for staying in the local church community and for spiritual direction, which is a very pastoral way of helping people know God in their pain. Let me also advocate for local counselors who have training in understanding the things that gum up our insides and leave us afraid.

Life change rarely happens fast or because of a general revelation. It usually happens because the Lord uses someone or something to get our specific attention and point us to specific steps towards growth. Not every counseling relationship is a fit, and it takes some hard work to process, pay for and continue in therapy.

If you need to work on something in your life that you are having a hard time working through, see it as your obedience to Christ to get some help. It will be less scary than you think it will be. It might also be more work than you think it might be. But, if you see it through with someone wise and prayerful, you might also grow much more than you thought was possible.

Joshua 4 Memorials

We are not just spiritual beings that float around and live in some ethereal Heaven snow globe. We are made of flesh and bone. We live in real life, real-time, with real schedules. We know that all of real life can be part of our spiritual life, but it takes some tangible physical things to help us hold on to that.

In Joshua 4, God leads the Israelites to cross the Jordan River, which he had miraculously stopped from flowing. Right after this, he instructs them to build an altar made of giant stones piled on top of each other. When the Israelites were walking near there for centuries to come they would see and remember the work of God.

It was just a pile of rocks.

But that intentional, physical, tangible pile of rocks reminded them of a lasting spiritual truth: Our God has been here and he can be with us again. Our God was and remains for us. Our God has delivered us before and can deliver us again.

As God deals with you over time, consider creating some type of memorial of what he has done. This could be a shelf with small trinkets on it. It could be a bracelet with beads on it that remind you of different life seasons of his faithfulness. It could be a shoebox that you pull out with tiny souvenirs of spiritual journeys that you have been on with Christ. It could be a tattoo sleeve that you add to over time. No face tattoos. That's weird.

If you haven't done this "over the years", you can do it now "for those years". Think of how you would want to do this. Consider a place where you would want to put these treasures left behind from the great journeys with God. Look over them. Let them remind you of what He has done before and so let him give you the courage he can do it again.

This is of such importance for the one who journeys through mental and emotional pain because the journey gets confusing. The steps are not very clear. The future is very overwhelming and it is so easy to feel lost. The tools for navigating the next steps are often through remembering who he was before. These memories of His faithfulness can be a compass and guide to stay on the path when we can no longer see the way easily.

In these times, we can not just say, "What do you want me to do?!" We can say, "Dear God, you have done it before, do it again."

Spiritual practices are the great friend of those seeking to know God in the midst of mental and emotional pain. They are practical pathways for us to wear down with Christ over time. When it is the darkest, it is the most difficult to navigate. Well trod paths offer great safety and bearing in the dark.

Vows for those who Practice Resurrection

Christ, you have vowed to me the gift of Your very resurrected self.
You have taken me to be your eternal companion
to have and to hold
for better, for worse,
for richer, for poorer,
in sickness and in health,
to love and to cherish,
till death delivers me into undimmed union forever with You

As I have been loved, so I learn to love.

I take you, Christ, to be my eternal companion
to have and to hold
for better, for worse,
for richer, for poorer,
in sickness and in health,
to love and to cherish,
till death delivers me into undimmed union forever with You

Help me live out these vows in my everyday reality
Transform me slow and thorough.
Protect me from feeling overwhelmed by my lack of practice up until now.
Free me from shame from feeling behind other practitioners
Lover of my soul, make yourself easy to see as I become more intentional to look
Develop spiritual muscles that survive the journey through the mire of darkness
Help me to work with my spiritual practice with you until it becomes native to my life, a joy to do, and a whole new way of existing together with you In the world.

[72] Eldridge, John. *Walking with God; How to Hear His Voice, Expanded Edition.* (Nashville, TN: Nelson Books, 2016).

[73] This is the headline of The Christian Leadership Institute's website. It also is lived out with a lot of intention with how they shape and practice their training. www.spiritualleadership.com. It is a wonderful community that gives room for God in a way that I have rarely experienced.

[74] Palmer, Parker J. *Let Your Life Speak; Listening for the Voice of Vocation.* (San Francisco, Jossey-Bass, 2000)

[75] I cannot find the source of the original way someone is supposed to do this prayer. Someone described it to me, and I modified it as an exercise based on the text in Hebrews 4. What is left of what that person originally told me or where she received it from are a mystery to me.

[76] This practice is often called *Lectio Divina.* It was introduced to me as *Morning Prayer.* This meditative way of listened to God through the Scripture is practiced in slightly different ways by whichever group or person that is facilitating it. The above is a way that I have found helpful to prioritize listening to the text and to give room to the voice and presence of God.

[77] Williams, Rowan. *Being Christian: Baptism, Bible, Eucharist, Prayer.* (Grand Rapids, MI: Eerdmans Publishing, 2014).

AFTERWORD

There is one story that I chose to not include in the book, but it has been with me while writing it. It is the story of Horatio Spafford. I did not include this story because it felt dissonant to speak of future fears, which is what Spafford brings up in me. We sufferers need to live in the present, not in the possible. But, in writing this book, I couldn't help but ask myself deeply personal and theological questions that were spawned by his story. It feels dishonest to not make mention of it somewhere. So, I stick in the Afterword, which few read anyway.

Horatio Spafford, as many readers will know, penned the lyrics to the beautiful hymn, It is Well with My Soul. He wrote this after experiencing a devastating tragedy in his life. He and his family were supposed to go on a trip to visit D.L. Moody, their friend and coworker in the faith, and hear him preach in England. Horatio was delayed on business and so sent his wife and four daughters ahead of him.

The ship carrying his family was struck by another boat. All four of his daughters died in the accident. His wife survived by floating on a piece of wood. Horatio came to be with his wife in England and followed the same path across the Atlantic Ocean as his perished children. When he was informed that he was at the very place where their boat sank, it is said that he began to pen the words to this great hymn.

The hymn is an anthem. It is a bold, articulate and faithful declaration of many of the truths that we have discussed in this book. It has been sung for over 100 years by sufferers who dare to proclaim God's goodness in the midst of the unfathomable dark.

What is less known is that Horatio Spafford later died in an insane asylum under the illusion that he was the Messiah.

I love this song, but this last part of the story was grievous to me. It was too sad for me. I think this is because of the devastation of his mental illness, along with the great loss he had already experienced. Even more so was the fact that this part of the story was not known or shared when the hymn's story was told in my environment. That part of the story didn't seem to fit in the narrative of God's kindness in suffering.

For years, this made the hymn more difficult for me to sing.

It made me confused that we could take his declaration of faith and tell part of his story and not include his mental illness and ultimate insanity. It made me wonder if Horatio himself would have changed his tune had he known that he would lose his mind.

But, like most of our big questions, this comes from a

personal place inside of me. We all have big hairy fears. Well, for someone who has OCD, Spafford lived out the nightmare that I hope I never have to. He ended his life in the way I desperately hope I will not end mine.

There were times in my life when I didn't know if I was going to make it. I didn't know I would be able to hold on - even to my sanity. For some people who have Obsessive Compulsive Disorder, it grows worse with age. For others, it doesn't. While OCD is not a psychotic disorder (as many would determine sanity), people with OCD can develop psychotic disorders. I live with a distant fear of it, and like all fears that obsess the mind, it is wisest to say, "It could be - I don't know," as opposed to trying to convince oneself one way or the other. Over the course of my life, I have had to come to accept that I cannot prove all of my fears false, including going mentally insane. I have not been given any promises from God that make me say that "it can never be me", which is exactly what my false self declares in pride and fear. The truth is, it could be me.

Horatio's story sent me into questions that I didn't have answers to. I questioned, would it still be well, then? Even lying in a hospital bed without the grace of lucidity. Would I be okay, there? What if my cross gets heavier? What if God lets it be more than I am able to walk with? Is he still good? Could, somehow, it still be well with me ... without much of me left?

I have learned that God is "even here" in my context of suffering. Is he "even there" in that loss of sanity?

I want to tell you that I actually sing the song from a deeper part of myself now. I have doubled down on loving and believing in the legacy of this hymn.

It gives far more comfort to me now than it did ever before.

I have come to believe that yes, even there. Even if I lose my mind, he will be with me. One could argue that there is less of "me" there in that scenario. But, whatever of me is left, he will not forsake. Even there His hand will hold me fast. Even there the nearness of God in abject suffering can create a wellness of soul. David writes that, "My flesh and my heart may fail, but God is the strength of my heart and my portion forever" (Psalm 73:26). I believe that is true for my mind as well.

Even there.

ACKNOWLEDGEMENTS

Many wives have husbands who are less afraid than they are. My wife didn't get one of those. Many wives have partners who help lead the adventure, calm the nerves, and dilute the tension with a non-anxious presence. She didn't get one of those either. The writing of this book plays out those things in vivid Colombian colors. I wrote this book while on a 3-month sabbatical from our church. We took the majority of that time to go to Adriana's birth country of Colombia and to physically meet her birth family that she had not seen since she was 8 months old. We did this with an 8-week-old baby. We ventured there in some sketchy Airbnb conditions, and my wife was quickly reminded of what type of husband she did marry. During this season, I had an OCD spike that had me battling minute-by-minute fears of financial ruin and disaster befalling our baby. I also took the leap to write this book. As she was taking care of the family, finding out her own birth story, taking care of an infant, and meeting many relatives, she encouraged me to take the time I needed to write. We often started our morning at 6 am looking at hummingbirds and talking over the content of the book. I knew it was an accurate chapter when I got her crying, as stories this close to home often do for us. She labors in love for me, for our children, and did that again for this book.

There are three couples that I sent the earliest chapters of this project. They are ones who have suffered in their own life and have been vital for me as I have struggled in mine. Without their encouragement and guidance, I would not have had the energy to continue, and I would not have had much of the perspective that is found in the pages. They are my parents, Mark and Marian Willey, and dear friends, Ralph and Ruth Reamer and Scott and Faith Parker. They have suffered holier and longer than I have, and I love the Christ that they reflect and speak of through their life stories.

Lisa Meyers has spent more time with this book than anyone besides my wife and me. She is a professor at Cairn University and has influenced and taught many people in our church how to write well. She graciously agreed to edit, proofread, and process through various parts of this with me. I work with Lisa on our Common Life team at Fellowship. We have produced devotional materials together over the last 7 years. They are a dear group of like-souled people who have spoken from their journey of faith and given of their time and talents to lead our church family with written materials. They also have discouraged me from using made-up words such as 'souled', but I am not asking for their help for this part. I have gotten input from many members of the team in the rest of the process.

Eric Rivera, Chris Katulka, Bob Stevenson, Joanne Sharp, Matt Miller, Joan Kings, Lisa Skopil, and Craig Babb have done me a great kindness in writing the reviews at the beginning of this book. Each of their lives and stories is one I deeply admire, and to have their perspective and encouragement is invaluable to me.

The Leadership Institute has had a tremendous influence on my adult life. They trained me in spiritual direction, but more than that, they taught me the language of prayer and the posture of listening. I highly recommend them and would be delighted if this helped point anyone their way. They offer *The Journey* and *The School for Spiritual Direction.*

There are two other special people that have had influence over this project although not direct involvement in it. The first is Harry Eason. He is a dear friend and has lived a life of a survivor through many physical and psychological hardships. He has taught me much about the heart of Christ and what it means to live an honest and messy life "with God". The other is my grandmother, Ellen Snyder. She has known the treasure of Jesus since before I have been alive. The conversations that I have had with her throughout the years have continually demonstrated that there is more to know, more to love, more to learn in my journey with Christ. I hope to be a butler in her mansions in glory one day.

Lastly, I want to mention the pastors that I serve with. None of them have Obsessive-Compulsive Disorder, and each of them has had to learn about it as they have ministered with me. They are whistleblowers for me when I am too stressed, endure with me when fear has too much of my ear, and love me when I need them as brothers and friends. Jerry Costolo, one of those dear pastors and friends, has encouraged me to write more than any other individual in my life. The dear pastors that have journeyed with me in this are Jesse Schmidt, Charles Moore, Keith McMinn, Mike Candy, Mark Willey, Chris Whorton, Tim Hunt, Jerry Costolo, Ralph Reamer, Don Loose, Andy Wallin, Scott Parker, Jim Panter, Jared Hacking, Joe Parker, and Ryan Anderson.

BIBLIOGRAPHY

Alcorn, Randy. *We Shall See God; Charles Spurgeon's Classic Devotional Thoughts on Heaven.* (Carol Stream, IL: Tyndale House Publishers Inc, 2011).

Amundsen, Dr. Darrel. "The Anguish and Agonies of Charles Spurgeon". Christian History Issue #29, 1991. Accessed https://christianhistoryinstitute.org/magazine/article/anguish-and-agonies-of-charles-spurgeon)

Biema, David Van. "Mother Teresa's Crisis of Faith." Tim Magazine, World. https://time.com/4126238/mother-teresas-crisis-of-faith/

Benner, David. *The Gift of Being Yourself; The Sacred Call to Self-Discovery.* (Downers Grove, IL: Intervarsity Press, 2015).

Buechner, Frederick. *Secrets in the Dark; A Life in Sermons.* (New York, NY: Harper Collins, 2006).

Cry, Jordan St. [Song] *Weary Traveler* 2021. CCLI #: 7184142

Calvin, John. *Institutes of the Christian Religion.* (Philadelphia: The Westminster Press, 1960.). He first published these in Latin in 1536 and later in French in 1541.

Eldridge, John. *Walking with God; How to Hear His Voice, Expanded Edition.* (Nashville, TN: Nelson Books, 2016).

Eswine, Zach. *Spurgeon's Sorrows. Realistic Hope for Those Who Suffer from Depression.* (Scotland, UK: Christian Focus Publications Ltd. 2014).

https://sojo.net/list-some-more-2000verses-scripture-poverty-and-justice

Hunter, James Davison. *The Irony, Tragedy and Possibility of Christianity in the Late Modern World.* (Walton Street, Oxford: Oxford University Press, 2010).

Hurnard, Hannah. *Hinds' Feet in High Places.* (Blacksburg, VA: Wilder Publications, 2010).

Kapic, Kelly M. *You're Only Human; How Your Limits Reflect God's Design and Why That's Good News.* (Grand Rapids, MI: Brazos Press, 2022)

Kapic, Kelly. "Take Time to be Unproductive: How Busyness can Waste A Life." *Desiring God Articles.* July 28, 2022. https://www.desiringgod.org/articles/take-time-to-be-unproductive

Larson, Gary. *Far Side Comic. "Just Plain Nuts."* (Seattle, WA: FarWorks, Inc, March 13, 1990).

Lewis, C.S. *The Problem of Pain.* (San Francisco: Harper One, 2015)

Lewis, C.S. *A Grief Observed.* (New York, NY: Harper Collins, 2015)

Lewis, CS. "First and Second Things". *God in the Dock: Essays on Theology and Ethics.* (Grand Rapids, MI: Eerdmans Publishing Company, 1994).

Mangold, James. *Indiana Jones and the Dial of Destiny.* [Film]. Walt Disney Pictures Lucasfilm Ltd. Released May 18, 2023.

McCarthy, Cormac. *The Road.* (New York, NY: Alfred A Knopf, 2006)

Moore, Beth. *All my Knotted-Up Life: A Memoir* (Carol Stream, IL: Tyndale 2023).

Mother Teresa; Come Be My Light; The Private Writings of the Saint of Calcutta. Edited and with Commentary by Kolodiejchuk, Brian M.C.(New York, NY: Double Day, 2007)

Noble, Alan. *On Getting out of Bed; The Burden and Gift of Living.* (Downers Grove: Intervarsity Press, 2023).

Nouwen, Henri. *The Wounded Healer: Ministry in Contemporary Society.* New York, NY: Doubleday, 1972.

Nouwen, Henri. *Bread for the Journey: A Day Book for Wisdom and Faith. San Francisco, CA*: Harper One, 2006).

Nouwen, Henri J.M. *Life of the Beloved: Spiritual Living in a Secular World.* (Crossroads Publishing, 2002)

Nouwen, Henri J. M. *The Inner Voice of Love: A Journey Through Anguish to Freedom. (*New York, NY: Image Books Doubleday, 1996.

Nouwen, Henri. *Return of the Prodigal Son: A Story of Homecoming.* New York, NY, 1994).

Ortberg, John. *Soul Keeping: Caring for the Most Important Part of You.* (Grand Rapids, MI: Zondervan, 2014).

Ortlund, Dane. *Gentle and Lowly: The Heart of Christ for Saints and Sinners* (Wheaton, IL: Crossway, 2020).

Packer, J.I. *A Quest for Godliness: The Puritan Vision of the Christian life.* (Wheaton, IL: Crossway Books, 1990)

Palmer, Parker J. *Let Your Life Speak; Listening for the Voice of Vocation.* (San Francisco, Jossey-Bass, 2000)

Peterson, Eugene. *Living the Resurrection: The Risen Christ in Everyday Life.* Colorado Springs, CO: Nav Press, 2020.

Redman, Matt. [Song] *One Day (When We All Get to Heaven).* CCLI 7091537.

Snyder, Albert C. *On a Hill Far Away; Journal of a Missionary Doctor in Rwanda.* (Minneapolis, MN: Light and Life Publishing, 1999)

Spurgeon, Charles. *Morning by Morning; or, Daily Readings For The Family of the Closet.* (New York: Robert Carter and Brothers, 1865).

Spurgeon, Charles. *Encouragement for the Depressed;* (Wheaton, IL: Crossway, 2020*).* They cited this: "From an address by Spurgeon on May 19, 1879. Cited in Ernest LeVos, C.H. Spurgeon and the Metropolitan Tabernacle (iUniverse, 2014).

Spurgeon, Charles, "Joy and Peace in Believing," *Metropolitan Tabernacle Pulpit (MTP),* Vol 12, Sermon 692 (http://www.spurgeonsgems.org/vols10-12/chs692.pdf), Accessed August 3rd, 2023.

Spurgeon, Charles Haddon. *Healing for the Wounded.* New Park Street Pulpit Volume 1. Accessed https://www.spurgeon.org/

resource-library/sermons/healing-for-the-wounded/

The Serenity Prayer is commonly attributed to Reinhold Niebuhr.

The Shorter Catechism with Scripture Proofs; The Westminster Assembly (New Zealand: Titus Books, 2014)

Taylor, Justin. "Charles Spurgeon's Battle with Depression". The Gospel Coalition Blogs: Evangelical History. May 19th, 2022. https://www.thegospelcoalition.org/blogs/evangelical-history/charles-spurgeons-battle-with-depression/

Tozer, A.W. *The Pursuit of God.* (Harrisburg, PA: Christian Publications, 1948)

Wiersbe, Warren. *Why Us? When Bad Things Happen to God's People.* (Grand Rapids, MI: Fleming H. Revell Company, 1984).

Wilburne, Rankin. Union With Christ: The Way to Know and Enjoy God. (Colorado Springs, CO: David C Cook, 2016.

Wilder, Jim. Renovated: God, Dallas Willard and the Church That Transforms. NavPress, Colorado Springs, 2020)

Williams, Rowan. *Being Christian: Baptism, Bible, Eucharist, Prayer.* (Grand Rapids, MI: Eerdmans Publishing, 2014).

Willard, Dallas. *The Divine Conspiracy: Rediscovering Our Hidden Life in God.* New York, NY: Harper One, 1998).

Made in the USA
Middletown, DE
02 February 2024

49032866R00116